MW01222110

QuickStudy®

for

American History

BarCharts, Inc.®

Boca Raton, Florida

DISCLAIMER:

This QuickStudy® Booklet is an outline only, and as such, cannot include every aspect of this subject. Use it as a supplement for course work and textbooks. BarCharts, Inc., its writers and editors are not responsible or liable for the use or misuse of the information contained in this booklet.

All rights reserved. No part of this publication may be reproduced or transmitted in any form or by any means, electronic or mechanical, including photocopy, recording, or any information storage and retrieval system, without written permission from the publisher.

©2006 BarCharts, Inc.

ISBN 13: 9781423200260

ISBN 10: 1423200268

BarCharts® and QuickStudy® are registered trademarks of BarCharts, Inc.

Publisher:

        BarCharts, Inc.

        6000 Park of Commerce Boulevard, Suite D

        Boca Raton, FL 33487

        www.quickstudy.com

Printed in Thailand

Contents

Contents

Study Hints

NOTE TO STUDENT:

This QuickStudy® booklet is designed as a timeline, with years set in blue for easy reference. Bullets set off the important events, people, terms, trends and other essential concepts.

Take your learning to the next level with QuickStudy®!

State abbreviations are used in many instances throughout this booklet:

Alabama (AL)	Montana (MT)
Alaska (AK)	Nebraska (NE)
Arizona (AZ)	Nevada (NV)
Arkansas (AR)	New Hampshire (NH)
California (CA)	New Jersey (NJ)
Colorado (CO)	New Mexico (NM)
Connecticut (CT)	New York (NY)
Delaware (DE)	North Carolina (NC)
Florida (FL)	North Dakota (ND)
Georgia (GA)	Ohio (OH)
Hawaii (HI)	Oklahoma (OK)
Idaho (ID)	Oregon (OR)
Illinois (IL)	Pennsylvania (PA)
Indiana (IA)	Rhode Island (RI)
Iowa (IA)	South Carolina (SC)
Kansas (KS)	South Dakota (SD)
Kentucky (KY)	Tennessee (TN)
Louisiana (LA)	Texas (TX)
Maine (ME)	Utah (UT)
Maryland (MD)	Vermont (VT)
Massachusetts (MA)	Virginia (VA)
Michigan (MI)	Washington (WA)
Minnesota (MN)	West Virginia (WV)
Mississippi (MS)	Wisconsin (WI)
Missouri (MO)	Wyoming (WY)

The New World
1492 – 1646

1492   ■ **Christopher Columbus** lands in the Bahamas.

1513   ■ **Ponce de Leon** lands in Florida.

1518   ■ Smallpox, brought by the Europeans, begins to decimate the native populations of Central and South America. The epidemic will last until 1530.

1521   ■ The surrender of **Tenochtitlan** (later, Mexico City) to Spanish explorer/conqueror **Ferdinand Cortes,** and the **Aztec** empire falls.

1533   ■ **Henry VIII** starts the English Reformation mainly to gain a divorce from Catherine of Aragon.

1539   ■ **Hernando de Soto** begins exploration of what will be the southeastern United States.

1540   ■ **Francisco Vasquez de Coronado** does the same in the southwest.

1558   ■ Henry VIII's daughter **Elizabeth I** becomes Queen of England.

1587 ■ **1587-90: Sir Walter Raleigh** starts, and fails, with a colony in **Roanoke** (an island off present-day North Carolina); the first attempt in North America.

1588 ■ The English navy, helped by violent storms, defeats the Spanish Armada.

1603 ■ **James I** becomes King of England.
■ **1603-05: Samuel de Champlain** of France explores what will be present-day Canada.

1607 ■ **Jamestown** (becomes Virginia) is founded.

1611 ■ The first Virginia tobacco crop is harvested.

1619 ■ The first African slaves arrive in Virginia.

1620 ■ **Plymouth Colony** (becomes Massachusetts) is founded.

1622 ■ The **Powhatan Confederacy** attacks the Virginia Colony.

1624 ■ The Dutch settle **Manhattan Island.**

1625 ■ **Charles I** becomes King of England.

1630 ■ The **Massachusetts Bay Colony** is founded.

1634   ■ **Maryland** is founded as a "haven for English Catholics."
       ■ **Roger Williams** is "expelled" from the Massachusetts Bay Colony, and founds **Providence** (becomes Rhode Island).

1636   ■ **Connecticut** is founded.

1637   ■ The **Pequot War** virtually wipes out the Pequot Indian tribe.
       ■ **Anne Marbury Hutchinson** and her followers are exiled to Rhode Island (from Massachusetts Bay Colony) for preaching what the Puritan elite call *heresy*.

1646   ■ **Virginia** and the **Powhatan Confederacy** sign a peace treaty.

2 A Society Forms

1642 – 1690

1642   ■ **1642-46:** The **English Civil War** sends many in search of the "New World."

1649   ■ **King Charles I** is executed.

1660   ■ The **House of Stuart** returns to the throne of England, and **King Charles II** rules.

1662   ■ The *"Halfway Covenant"* is drafted in Massachusetts:
- Adults who had been baptized but were not full church members could have their children baptized if they recognized Church authority and lived by its precepts.
- They could not, however, vote or take communion.

1663   ■ **Carolina** is chartered, then split into two: north and south.

1664   ■ England defeats the Dutch and takes over New Amsterdam, naming it **New York.**

1675   ■ **"King Philip's War"**
- **Chief Metacomet** ("King Philip") of **Pokanet** tribe rises against Pilgrim encroachment of tribal lands.
- Destroys 12 of 90 Puritan towns.
- Lack of food and ammunition brings about defeat.
- Metacomet killed. Tribe virtually wiped out except in Martha's Vineyard area.

1676   ■ **Bacon's Rebellion** in Virginia
- Farmer **Nathaniel Bacon** rouses farmers to fight Indians.
- **Governor William Berkeley** declares him "in rebellion."
- Bacon marches on Jamestown and burns capitol to the ground. When he dies of dysentery, the rebellion collapses.

■ **Pueblo Revolt**
- Led by Medicine Man **Pope** ("po-pay"), **Pueblos** in **New Mexico** revolt against Spaniards and drive them out.
- Spaniards out of power until 1692, when they engender new spirit of cooperation with native tribes.

■ Maryland colonists, "forced" to eat the oysters along their shore to keep from starvation, found a new industry.

1681   ■ **Pennsylvania** is chartered.

1682   ■ **James II** becomes King of England.

1686   ■ **Dominion of New England** is formed.
- Charters of all individual states revoked due to "non-English" practices.
- **Sir Edmund Andros** is named Governor of Dominion.

1688   ■ **James II** is deposed in the **"Glorious Revolution."**
- **William and Mary** gain the throne.

1689   ■ Dominion of New England is overthrown.
- Andros is jailed.
- Return to former state charters hoped for but not achieved.

■ **"King William's War"**
- AKA: The War of the League of Augsburg
- Americans fight on northern frontiers.
- Many colonies are decimated.
- Ends in 1697.

1690   ■ **John Locke** writes an *Essay Concerning Human Rights*, a major contribution to the era known as **"The Enlightenment."**

3

A Country Grows

1691 – 1770

1691   ■ The **Massachusetts Colony** gets a new charter giving it all North American Territories north to the St. Lawrence River.

1692   ■ **Salem Witchcraft Hysteria**
- Started as a "prank" by a group of adolescent girls.
- Nineteen people are executed; hundreds are imprisoned.

1693   ■ The **College of William and Mary** is founded in the Virginia Colony.

1695   ■ The city of **Annapolis** is laid out in Maryland to serve as the colonial capital.

1696   ■ **The Board of Trade and Plantations**, the chief organ of British Government with respect to the American Colonies, is established.

1701   ■ The city of **Detroit** is founded as the French settlement Fort Pontchatrain on a strait between Lake Erie and Lake St. Clair.

1702   ■ **"Queen Anne's War"** AKA: The War of the Spanish Succession begins. (Will end in 1713.)
   • Although placing a heavy economic burden on colonies, has less effect than "King William's War."

1711   ■ **Tuscarora War** begins in North Carolina. (Will end in 1713.)
   • Tuscarora tribe was trading members of other tribes as slaves.
   • These tribes joined English to fight against them.

1715   ■ **Yamasee War** in South Carolina is a protest against English mistreatment and slavery.

1720   ■ Smallpox epidemic hits Boston.
   • **Cotton Mather** urges citizens to try new technique called *inoculation.*
   • Those that get inoculated survive in five times greater numbers.

1720   ■ **1720-40:** The Black population of Chesapeake grows substantially through natural increase.

1732   ■ **Georgia** is chartered.

1739   ■ Slaves in the **Stono River** area of South Carolina arm themselves and rebel.
   • Head for Florida, hoping for refuge in the Spanish Colony.
   • Militia puts down rebellion in a day.

- All Blacks involved are killed immediately or executed subsequently.

■ **"King George's War"** begins with Spain.

- Combined with Stono Rebellion, this feeds fears of whites against Black uprising and leads to a reign of terror in New York against imagined "conspirators."

- War will end in 1748.

1765 ■ The **Hudson River Land Riots** of squatters against powerful landowners lead to an almost year-long control of the Hudson River Valley by insurgents.

1767 ■ **"Regulator"** movement starts in South Carolina. (Will end in 1769.)

- Essentially a vigilante movement against perceived lax law enforcement.

- Will spawn a "regulator" movement in North Carolina, ending with **Battle of Alamance** in 1771.

1770 ■ 21-year-old Boston printer **Isaiah Thomas** begins publication of the *Massachusetts Spy*, one of the earliest pro-colonist/anti-British newspapers.

4

The Seeds of Revolution

1754 – 1774

1754   ■ **Albany Congress** is convened by delegates from seven British northern and middle colonies in response to French activities on the western frontiers.
  • It attempts to convince Iroquois to abandon neutrality and join the English, and to coordinate colonial defenses. Both goals fail.

■ **French and Indian War** begins.

1760   ■ British dismissal of abilities of colonial soldiers in the French and Indian War leads to a furthering of dissension between colonies and home country.
■ **George III** becomes King of England.

1763   ■ *Treaty of Paris* is signed.
  • France cedes all major North American holdings to England.
  • Spain cedes Florida.

■ **Pontiac**, war chief of an Ottawa village near Detroit, unites tribes and lays siege to a Detroit fort while his troops attack other British outposts in the region.

■ *Proclamation of 1763* "apologizes" the Indians for encroachment and declares a strict temporary boundary for colonial settlement.

1764   ■ *Sugar Act,* designed specifically to enrich England, raises new duties on imports to the New World, infuriating the colonists.

1765   ■ *Stamp Act* imposes a heavy tax on colonies.
   - The **Sons of Liberty** is formed to unite colonials in opposition to the taxes. Some of the protests get violent.

1766   ■ Stamp Act is repealed, but *Declaratory Act* asserts Britain's ability to tax and legislate for American possessions "in all cases whatsoever."

1767   ■ *Townshend Acts* impose greater taxes on colonies.

1770   ■ **Lord North** becomes **Prime Minister** of Britain.
   ■ Townshend Acts are repealed—except the tax on tea.

   ■ **Boston Massacre** lights the fuse on American resentment at its highest.

1772   ■ **Boston Committee of Correspondence** urges immediate boycott of all British goods.

1773   ■ *Tea Act* eliminates colonial middlemen and their profits from tea trade.
   - Leads directly to **Boston Tea Party.**

1774   ■ *Coercive Acts*, (*"Intolerable Acts"*) are implemented by Lord North, fanning the flames of revolution.

The Revolution
1774 – 1783

1774 ■ **First Continental Congress** is convened.

1775 ■ **Lord Dunmore's** proclamation is issued. In a letter to **General Thomas Gage,** Dunmore downplays any chance of significant revolution from "rude rabble without a plan."

■ **Battles of Lexington and Concord** are fought; **Revolutionary War** officially begins.

■ **Second Continental Congress** is convened. Originally intended as "interim," it becomes, in essence, the country's seat of government.

1776 ■ **Thomas Paine** writes *Common Sense*, rallying Americans.

■ The British evacuate Boston.

■ **Thomas Jefferson** writes, and the Congress signs, the *Declaration of Independence.*

• Anti-slavery clauses omitted due to Southern pressure.

■**Battle for New York City** is fought.
- **General George Washington** proves a formidable foe.
- Delays on British side add to America's strength.

1777 ■The British capture **Philadelphia.**
■British **General Burgoyne** surrenders at **Saratoga** (New York).

1778 ■France joins the battle on America's side.
■The British evacuate Philadelphia.

1779 ■**General John Sullivan** leads an expedition against the **Iroquois** for their support of British forces; all crops, orchards and settlements are destroyed.

1780 ■British control **Charleston** (South Carolina).

1781 ■British **General Cornwallis** surrenders at **Yorktown.**
1782 ■Peace negotiations begin in Paris.

1783 ■*Treaty of Paris* gives America unconditional independence and establishes America's boundaries, while ignoring territorial claims of native tribes.

6

A Nation Is Formed

1776 – 1788

1776 ■ **Second Continental Congress** directs each state to draft an individual constitution.
■ North Carolina extends its jurisdiction by annexing the Watagua settlement, now calling it **Washington County.**

1777 ■ *Articles of Confederation* forming the "united" states are sent to the states for ratification.
■ New Connecticut "republic" renames itself **Vermont**, and adopts a constitution mandating suffrage for all men and banning slavery.

1778 ■ Sandwich Islands (later to become the state of **Hawaii)** are discovered by **Captain James Cook.**

1779 ■ The first written report on the planting and use of sweet corn (discovered along the Susquehanna River) is published.

1780 ■ To control rampant inflation, Congress passes the *"40 to 1" Act*, stating that continental paper money will be redeemed at one-fortieth ($\frac{1}{40}$) of its face value. The phrase "...not worth a continental" enters common speech.

1781   ■ **Articles of Confederation** are ratified.

1782   ■ **Congress** adopts the Great Seal of the United States.

1783   ■ **Virginia House of Burgesses** grants freedom to any Black slaves who served in the Continental Army.
        ■ **George Washington** issues his "Farewell Address to the Army," and all troops are formally discharged.
        ■ **Noah Webster** publishes *Webster's Spelling Book*, codifying American words and spelling for the first time.
          • In 1828 he will publish *An American Dictionary of the English Language.*

1784   ■ The British transport all **Acadians** to Maine and Louisiana, where, combining their Canadian origins with the "injun" style of life and cookery, they become known as **"Cajuns."**

1785   ■ Congress establishes the ***dollar*** as the official U.S. currency, using a decimal system devised by Thomas Jefferson.

1786   ■ **Annapolis Convention** is held to discuss U.S. trade policies.
          • Eight states name representatives, but only five attend.
          • Another convention is called for in Philadelphia in nine months.

■ Farmer **Daniel Shays** leads a rebellion against high taxes and low money supply in western Massachusetts. Because Shays and many others involved are "gentlemen" (i.e., landowners), government is forced to rethink policies.

1787 ■ *Northwest Ordinance* guarantees settlers in the Northwest Territories many of the freedoms later to be incorporated into the *Bill of Rights*.

■ **Constitutional Convention** convenes.

- The *Constitution of the United States* is signed on September 17.

- Benjamin Franklin states: "…there are several parts of the constitution which I do not… approve (but) I expect no better and I am not sure that it is not the best."

1788 ■ **James Madison, John Jay** and **Alexander Hamilton** urge New York's (and the nation's) ratification of the *Federalist,* which explains the meaning of the Constitution and assures immediate addition of *Bill of Rights.*

■ The Constitution is ratified.

7

The Early Republic

1789 – 1800

1789
■ **George Washington** is inaugurated as the first president.

■ *Judiciary Act* provides for a **Supreme Court** of six members, including a Chief Justice and five associate justices.

- Defines jurisdiction of the federal judiciary.
- Establishes 13 district courts and 3 circuit courts of appeal.

■ **United States House of Representatives** holds its first meeting on April 1; 30 days before George Washington assumes the office of president.

■ **French Revolution** begins.

■ Congress passes the first *Tariff Act.*

■ 12 *Amendments* are proposed to the Constitution.

■ **Georgetown University** has its beginnings.

■ The first American advertisement for tobacco appears.

■ Baptist minister **Elijah Craig** distills the first bourbon whiskey in the Kentucky region.

■ Nine out of 10 Americans are engaged in farming and food production.

1790   ■ **Secretary of the Treasury Alexander Hamilton** issues the first ***Report on Public Credit,*** aiming to expand financial reach of federal government and reduce power of the states.

■ The House of Representatives votes to locate the nation's capital on a 10-mile stretch along the Potomac River.

■ The first successful U.S. cotton mill is established in what will later become Pawtucket, Rhode Island.

■ Congress establishes the first U.S. Patent Office.

1791   ■ ***Bill of Rights*** becomes U.S. law, with Virginia's ratification.

■ The Bill of Rights is ratified.

■ Vermont becomes the 14th state to enter the union.

1792   ■ **Eli Whitney** invents the cotton gin.

■ **Thomas Paine** publishes the *Rights of Man,* arguing that power should rest with the democratic majority.

1793   ■ **President Washington** meets, at his home, with the heads of his departments of **State, Treasury,** and **War,** the **Attorney General** and the **Postmaster General,** thereby holding the first "cabinet" meeting.

■ France declares war on Britain, Spain, and Holland; U.S. remains neutral.

■ **Democratic-Republican Societies,** sympathetic to French cause, are founded.

■ **Thomas Jefferson** resigns as Secretary of State to head the anti-federalist Democratic-Republican Party.

■ Congress passes the *Fugitive Slave Act.*

1794 ■ The **Whiskey Rebellion** against high taxes leads Washington to send troops to Pennsylvania to avoid repeat of Shays Rebellion.

■ **Battle of Fallen Timbers** (Ohio Territory), led by General "Mad" Anthony Wayne, defeats native tribes demanding territorial rights and opens way for negotiations on settlement of the area.

■ America's first trade union, **The Federal Society of Journeymen Cordwainers** (shoemakers) is organized.

1795 ■ The *Jay Treaty* resolves issues of Anglo-American affairs, averting war.

■ First railroad in America, a wooden railed tramway running the slope of Beacon Hill, is built in Boston.

■ *Treaty of Greenville* signed by Wayne and delegates from the Miami Confederacy; gives U.S. right to settle the Ohio Territory.

1796 ■ The first contested presidential election is held.

　• **John Adams** (Federalist Party) is elected.

　• **Thomas Jefferson** (Republican) is vice president.

■The Supreme Court rules on the constitutionality of an act of Congress for the first time: *Hylton v. United States.*

1797 ■First ship of the **United States Navy**, called, appropriately, the *United States*, is launched.

1798 ■The **"XYZ Affair"** shows France treating America with disdain and leads to wave of anti-French sentiment.

■*Alien and Sedition Acts,* four laws designed by Federalists to prevent dissent and the growth of the Republican Party, are passed.

■*Virginia and Kentucky Resolutions* repudiate the Alien and Sedition Acts.

■Congress establishes the Marine Hospital Service, which will later become the *U.S. Public Health Service.*

■Eli Whitney pioneers the "American System" of mass production to build firearms.

■The first professional American writer, **Charles Brockden Brown,** publishes *Alcuin: A Dialogue on the Rights of Women.*

1799 ■Charles Brockden Brown publishes *Arthur Mervyn,* the first novel to use distinctly American characters and settings.

■U.S. and France engage in undeclared war in the West Indies (a.k.a. "The Quasi-War").

■ **George Washington** dies.

- **General Henry ("Lighthorse Harry") Lee** delivers a eulogy declaring Washington "First in war, first in peace, and first in the hearts of his countrymen."

1800 ■ **Franco-American Convention** ends the Quasi-War and frees U.S. from obligations to France from the *Treaty of 1778.*

■ **Thomas Jefferson** is elected president. **Aaron Burr** is vice president.

■ **Gabriel's Rebellion** is a Black revolt in Virginia, led by Gabriel Prosser, where the participants demand equal rights.

■ Congress passes the *Public Land Act* (a.k.a. the *Harrison Land Act*), providing liberal credit terms for land purchase and encouraging speculation in real estate and expansion.

■ **Parson Mason Locke Weems** publishes his *Life of Washington.*

- Any resemblance to the actual life of the president is purely accidental.
- The "cherry tree" fable is included.

Liberty Grows
1801 – 1823

8

1801
- **John Marshall** named **Chief Justice** of the Supreme Court.
- **President Thomas Jefferson** refuses to pay tribute to the Sultan of Tripoli (Africa) to protect U.S. ships from Barbary Pirates.

1803
- Navy begins blockade of Tripoli Harbor.
- *Marbury v. Madison* establishes the Supreme Court's power to judge constitutionality of issues.
- **Louisiana Purchase** (877,000 square miles) expands U.S. territories westward, doubling the size of the country.

1804
- Marines march into the port of Derna (Tripoli).
- **Thomas Jefferson** is re-elected.
- **Lewis and Clark** expedition begins. It will end in 1806, with information on vast territories in the northwest.

1805
- Peace treaty signed in Tripoli.

1807
- *Chesapeake Affair* exposes U.S. military weakness, as British ship destroys U.S. *Chesapeake* in U.S. territorial waters.
- *Embargo Act* forbids all U.S. exports and virtually eliminates imports.

1808   ■ **James Madison** is elected president.

1812   ■ **War of 1812** begins (U.S. v. Britain).

1814   ■ *Treaty of Ghent* on Christmas Eve halts hostilities.
       ■ **Hartford Convention** sees conservatives attempting to limit the powers of the president and radically change the Constitution.

1815   ■ Andrew Jackson becomes a hero at **Battle of New Orleans**.

1816   ■ **James Monroe** is elected president.
       ■ Second Bank of the United States is chartered.

1817   ■ *Rush-Bagot Treaty* leads to the demilitarization of the U.S./Canadian border.

1819   ■ In *McCulloch v. Maryland,* Chief Justice John Marshall establishes that the Supreme Court supersedes state courts in matters of Federal rights.
       ■ *Adams-Onis Treaty* cedes Florida to the U.S. and sets U.S. southern border.

1820   ■ *Missouri Compromise* prohibits slavery in Louisiana Territory states north of Missouri's southern boundary.
       ■ Monroe is re-elected.

1823   ■ *Monroe Doctrine* declares "most of the Western Hemisphere" off limits to foreign (European) intervention.

American Growth
1805 – 1857

9

1805   ■ Shawnee Chiefs **Prophet and Tecumseh** emerge as leaders preaching a united front against U.S. encroachment and military might. They will align with the British in the **War of 1812.**

1807   ■ **Robert Fulton** presents the first steamboat, the *Clermont*.

1810   ■ **New York City** surpasses Philadelphia in population.

1813   ■ Tecumseh dies, as does hope of a united front against U.S. treaty policies.
        ■ **Boston Manufacturing Company** is founded.
        • Uses the first American power loom, which radically changes textile manufacturing.
        • Combines all manufacturing processes under one roof.

1818   ■ **National Road,** a stone-based, gravel-top highway beginning in Cumberland, Maryland, reaches Wheeling, Virginia (now WV). It will reach Columbus, Ohio, by 1833.

1819   ■ *Indian Civilization Act* is passed, aimed at assimilating tribes into the white mainstream through government financial aid and boarding schools.

■ *Dartmouth College v. Woodward* establishes noninterference by states in commerce and business where a "contract" exists.

1820   ■ **1820 and beyond**—New England textile mills expand and dominate the market.

1824   ■ **President James Monroe** proposes removal of all native tribes to lands west of the Mississippi, an "honorable" move to assure the tribes' right to dwell in peace.

■ *Gibbons v. Ogden:* Supreme Court ends monopoly on steamboat trade by ruling that Congress, not individual states, controls commerce as per the "commerce clause" of the Constitution.

1827   ■ *Freedom's Journal*, the first Black weekly, begins publication.

1830   ■ **Baltimore & Ohio Railroad** starts operating.

1831   ■ *Cherokee Nation v. Georgia* attempts to fight Monroe's removal policy through legal means.
        • **Chief Justice John Marshall** rules that Indians are neither a foreign nation nor a state, and so have no standing in a federal court.

■ **Trail of Tears** begins when the Choctaw (native tribes of Mississippi and Alabama) are forced to lands west of the Mississippi.

■ Cyrus McCormick invents the **McCormick Reaper**, vastly improving farm productivity and efficiency.

1832   ■ **Chief Justice Marshall** clarifies his position regarding the Cherokee by stating that their Nation is a distinct political community, in which the "laws of the state of Georgia can have no force."

 • Further, forbids Georgians from entering without permission or treaty privilege.

 • This is ignored, and the Trail of Tears continues.

1834   ■ Due to "unfair practices" at the Lowell (MA) textile mills, the mill workers, all women, "turn out" (i.e., go on strike). The strike is unsuccessful and leads to even greater pressures on workers.

1835   ■ **Seminole War** erupts. Led by **Osceola,** the Seminoles will battle until 1842.
■ **Erie Canal** is completed.

1837   ■ The city of Boston employs paid policemen.
■ A potato famine starts in Ireland, leading to mass Irish immigration—1.3 million by 1857.
■ *Charles River Bridge v. Warren Bridge* establishes that new enterprises cannot be restricted by implied privileges under old charters to which they were not party.

1839   ■ An economic depression begins, lasting until 1843.

1844   ■ Baltimore-Washington telegraph line is established.

1848   ■ An abortive revolution in Germany is the impetus for German immigration—1.1 million by 1857.
        ■ The discovery of gold at Sutter's Mill (CA) starts the great **California "Gold Rush."**

1849   ■ A theater riot erupts in New York:
        • As theaters were the place where people of all classes and races mixed in the same building, they became the arenas for "class wars."

        • This riot is culmination of many smaller ones starting as early as 1830.

1853   ■ The British begin a study of the American manufacturing system.

1854   ■ The railroad reaches the Mississippi River.

1857   ■ A new depression begins.

10

Expansion & Reform

1825 – 1848

1825   ■ The House of Representatives elects **John Quincy Adams** president.

■ Adams delivers the first presidential message to Congress, urging growth, reform, establishment of a national university system, and an astronomical observatory in Washington.

■ 600 Boston carpenters go on strike, arguing for a 10-hour workday in U.S.

■ Fur trader Pierre Cabanne opens a trading post on the Missouri River, which will become **Omaha** (NE).

■ **General Simon Perkins** founds **Akron** (OH).

1826   ■ **American Society for the Promotion of Temperance** is founded to defeat "demon rum."

■ Anti-Masonry becomes an organized movement when disillusioned Mason, William Morgan, writes an "exposé" *The Illustration of Masonry by One of the Fraternity Who Has Devoted Thirty Years to the Subject.*

■The first overland journey to Southern California leaves Great Salt Lake on August 22, arrives in San Diego on November 27.

■**Gideon B. Smith** plants first Chinese mulberry trees in U.S., giving impetus to silk trade.

■**Lyceum Movement** led by Josiah Holbrook spreads interest in the arts, sciences, and "public issues" throughout the eastern U.S.

1827   ■**Creek Nation** cedes its western Georgia lands to the U.S.

1828   ■Passage of *Tariff of Abominations* leads southern states to devise the *Doctrine of Nullification,* giving states the right to overrule federal legislation in conflict with their own.

■**Andrew Jackson** is elected president.

■Construction begins on the **Baltimore & Ohio Railroad.**

■**Delaware and Hudson Canal** opens, linking Kingston with Port Jervis (both in NY)—where it connects with the Lackawanna Canal to Honesdale (PA)— a distance of 108 miles.

1829   ■**American Society for Encouraging Settlement in Oregon** is established in Boston after Congress defeats a bill to set up a territorial government there.

1830   ■ The **Webster-Hayne Debates** discuss the notion of nullification and the meaning of "union."

■ A second (political) party system begins to develop.

1831   ■ *Liberator,* an anti-slavery journal, begins publication.

■ The first national **Anti-Mason Convention** is held.

1832   ■ **Andrew Jackson** vetoes rechartering of the Second Bank of the United States.

■ Jackson is re-elected president.

1833   ■ Americans living in **Texas** vote to separate from Mexico.

1834   ■ The U.S. government demands Seminoles leave Florida as per an 1832 treaty.

1835   ■ Mexico proclaims a unified constitution that abolishes slavery. U.S. citizens living in Texas vote to secede, rather than give up this right.

1836   ■ **Republic of Texas** is established.

■ To end public land monopoly of speculators and capitalists, the *Specie Circular* states that only specie (gold or silver) or Virginia land scrip is acceptable payment for land.

■ **Martin Van Buren** is elected president.

1837   ■ A financial panic hits the U.S.
■ Tensions rise along the U.S./Canada border.

■ **Horace Mann** is named first head of the Massachusetts Board of Education, a position he will hold until 1848.

1838   ■ **Underground Railroad** is organized by abolitionists to provide slaves an escape route to the North.

1839   ■ U.S. enters a depression that will last until 1843.

1840   ■ **William Henry Harrison** (Whig Party) wins presidency.

1841   ■ **Brook Farm**, a cooperative that rejects materialism and seeks satisfaction in communal life, founded by Unitarian Minister George Ripley.
■ Upon Harrison's death (after less than a month in office) **John Tyler** becomes president.

■ Missionaries report the "wonders" of the **Oregon Territory** leading to "Oregon Fever" for expansion.

1843   ■ European support for an independent Texas causes U.S. interest.

1844   ■ **James Polk** is elected president.

1845   ■ **Texas** joins the union.

1847 ■ **Mormons** arrive in Utah Territory.
■ First Chinese immigrants arrive in New York.

1848 ■ **Women's Rights Convention** is held in Seneca Falls, NY.
■ New York becomes base for the **Cunard Steamship Line**, making it the center of European travel to and from the New World.
■ A telegraph line opens from New York to Chicago.
■ The **Oneida Community**, the first communal society in the U.S., is formed in central New York.
■ Pennsylvania enacts a child labor law restricting workers' age.

Slavery
1712 – 1865

1712 ■ A Black insurrection is staged in New York; 21 Blacks are executed.
■ **Pennsylvania Colony** enacts legislation banning the importation of slaves.

1713 ■ England's **South Sea Company** is granted permission to import 4,800 slaves per year into the Spanish colonies of North America for a period of 30 years.

1716 ■ First **Black slaves** arrive in French territory of Louisiana.

1724 ■ **French Louisiana Governor de Bienville** establishes a code to regulate behavior of Blacks.

1725 ■ Slave population is estimated at 75,000.

■ Right to a separate Black Baptist Church granted in Williamsburg (VA).

1731 ■ An English order prohibits implementing duty on imported slaves by the colonial legislatures.

1735   ■ Colonist **John Van Zandt** (NY) horse-whips his slave so severely that the slave dies, and a coroner's jury attributes the death to a "visitation of God."

1739   ■ Three separate Black insurrections occur in South Carolina.

1740   ■ A planned revolt by Charleston (SC) slaves revealed; 50 slaves hanged.

1741   ■ **New York City Panic** based on unfounded fears of a Black uprising leads to 18 Blacks hanged, 13 burned to death, and 70 banished.

1743   ■ New Jersey clergyman **John Woolman** preaches against slavery.

1749   ■ **Georgia Colony** revokes a prohibition against slavery, giving it legal recognition and starting the plantation system.

1772   ■ In the *Sommersett Case,* **Chief Justice Lord Mansfield** declares a slave free the moment he sets foot on English soil.

1773   ■ Yale President **Ezra Stiles** and clergyman **Samuel Hopkins** propose colonizing West Africa with freed slaves.

1775   ■ Benjamin Franklin and Dr. Benjamin Rush establish the **Society for the Relief of Free Negroes Unlawfully Held in Bondage.**

1780   ■ The Pennsylvania legislature mandates the gradual abolition of slavery within the state.

1788 ■ The Massachusetts legislature enacts a bill making slave trade illegal.

1790 ■ The **Society of Friends** (Quakers) presents to Congress the first petition calling for the abolition of slavery.

1791 ■ **Slave uprising in Haiti** leads to slave revolt in Spanish Louisiana.

1792 ■ Clergyman **David Rice** fails in his attempt to get the Kentucky constitutional convention to outlaw slavery.
■ Virginia statesman **George Mason** leads his state's opposition to slavery.

1793 ■ Congress enacts the *Fugitive Slave Act.*

1794 ■ Congress bans slave trade with foreign nations.

1799 ■ New York passes a gradual emancipation law.

1800 ■ **Gabriel's Rebellion,** a slave revolt, explodes in Virginia.

1808 ■ Congress passes legislation forbidding foreign slave trade.

1816 ■ Clergyman Robert Finley founds **The American Colonization Society** to resettle freed slaves in Africa. Establishes the Republic of **Liberia.**

1820   ■ *Missouri Compromise* is established.
        ■ Congress makes trade in foreign slaves an "act of piracy."

1821   ■ **Benjamin Lundy** publishes the *Genius of Universal Emancipation*, one of the earliest abolition journals.

1822   ■ A planned slave revolt in Charleston (SC) by freed Black **Denmark Vesey** is thwarted.

1830   ■ A schooner out of Virginia, bound for New Orleans, is wrecked off the Bahamas. British authorities declare the slaves it was carrying free.

1832   ■ **Virginia Assembly** debates abolition.

1836   ■ The **Massachusetts State Supreme Court** frees any slave brought across the state border.

1837   ■ Frederick Douglass escapes to freedom and becomes first "fugitive slave" lecturer speaking in America and abroad, and leading equal rights demonstrations.

1841   ■ **U.S. Supreme Court** rules that 53 Black mutineers from the Spanish slave ship *Amistad,* who had been taken into U.S. custody, shall be free to return to Africa.

1845   ■ *Narrative of the Life of Frederick Douglass* is published, followed by establishment of the newspaper *North Star.*

1850   ■ Practice of selling slaves to new and less "comfortable" plantations further south along the Mississippi causes the expression **"sold down the river"** to enter American language.

1859   ■ Georgia passes a law banning wills or deeds granting freedom to slaves, and enacts legislation allowing any Black indicted for vagrancy to be sold.
       ■ **President James Buchanan** opposes slave trade, yet bans searches of U.S. ships by British patrols, thus giving virtual immunity to continue the trade.

1861   ■ **Civil War** begins.
       ■ Northern states have a population of over 22 million.
       ■ The Confederacy has 10 million, of which over one-third are slaves.

1862   ■ Congress abolishes slavery in District of Columbia and U.S. Territories.

1863   ■ *Emancipation Proclamation* frees slaves *only* in those states at war against the Union.

1865   ■ **Civil War** ends.
       ■ *Thirteenth Amendment,* freeing slaves in both North and South, is ratified.

The Road West— To War

1846 – 1861

1846 ■ **Mexican-American War** begins over Texas borders and lands west that **President James Polk** wants for U.S.

■ **Representative David Wilmot** offers an amendment to a war appropriations bill: "… neither slavery nor involuntary servitude shall ever exist …" in territories won from Mexico. It fails but becomes the rallying cry for "Free Soilers" and abolitionists.

1847 ■ Presidential nominee **General Lewis Cass** proposes **Popular Sovereignty** (each territory to decide whether to be "slave" or "free").

1848 ■ **Zachary Taylor** is elected president.

1849 ■ **California** applies for statehood.

1850   ■ *Compromise of 1850,* devised by **Senators Henry** ("The Great Pacificator") **Clay** and **Stephen A.** ("The Little Giant") **Douglas**, admits California as a free state, gives New Mexico and Utah territories power to legislate "all rightful subjects … consistent with the Constitution" (i.e., slavery), and promises stronger fugitive slave laws and suppression of slave trade in the District of Columbia.

1852   ■ **Harriet Beecher Stowe's** *Uncle Tom's Cabin* is published and influences anti-slavery feelings. **Abraham Lincoln** will call Stowe "The little lady who started the war."
        ■ **Franklin Pierce** is elected president.

1854   ■ *Kansas-Nebraska Act* repeals slavery limitations set by the *Missouri Compromise,* allowing Kansas and Nebraska territories to be slave owning if they so choose. In the *Appeal of the Independent Democrats,* six congressman call this "a gross violation of a sacred pledge."
        ■ **Republican Party** is formed and makes inroads against the Democrats in congressional elections.

1856   ■ Battles over slavery in **Kansas** earn it the nickname "Bleeding Kansas."
        ■ **Senator Charles Sumner** (MA) denounces the "crime against Kansas," and is brutally beaten on the Senate floor by **Representative Preston Brooks** (SC).
        ■ **James Buchanan** is elected president.

1857   ■ ***Dred Scott v. Sanford*** effectively voids the ***Missouri Compromise.***
- Scott, a Missouri slave, had sued for freedom, stating that he had been taken so frequently into free territory that he was a resident there.
- Supreme Court rules Scott "not a citizen"; therefore, not free, and, in any event, Congress could not bar slavery from a territory.

■ ***Lecompton Constitution*** (KS) permits slavery. It is defeated in 1858 after anti-slavery forces are elected to the majority.

1858   ■ Presidential nominee **Stephen A. Douglas** (D) begins a series of cross-country debates with nominee **Abraham Lincoln** (R).
- Douglas's ***Freeport Doctrine*** states that territorial legislatures can bar slavery either by passing such a law or not enforcing slavery laws.

■ **Iowa State College** and **Oregon State University** are founded.

1859   ■ Abolitionist **John Brown** stages raid on **Harpers Ferry (VA)** in hopes of starting slave revolt. It fails.

1860   ■ **Democratic Party splits.** Southern members walk out of the nominating convention to protest Douglas's mollifying "free" states.

■ **Abraham Lincoln** is elected president.

■ *Crittenden Compromise,* to re-establish the principles of the *Missouri Compromise,* fails.

■ **South Carolina secedes** from the Union.

1861   ■ Mississippi, Florida, Alabama, Georgia, Louisiana and Texas pass secession ordinances and form the **Confederate States of America (CSA)**, electing **Jefferson Davis** as president.

■ **Kansas** enters the Union as a free state.

■ **Abraham Lincoln** sends a supply ship into South Carolina territorial waters to bring food to **Fort Sumter** in Charleston harbor. Given a choice between an attack on the fort or submission, the Carolinians attack.

■ **Civil War/War Between the States** has begun.

13

The War
1861 – 1865

1861 ■ All southern states except **Missouri, Kentucky, Maryland, Delaware and western Virginia** secede.

■ **Battle of Bull Run**, named for a stream near **Manassas Junction** (VA), shows that the war is very real and bloody.

- South wins when 9,000 additional troops under **General Thomas Jackson** arrive.

- During the battle, a spectator remarked that, amid all the chaos, Jackson is standing "firm as a stone wall."

- Many Southerners refer to battle as the first **Battle of Manassas.**

■ **General George McClellan** organizes an expanded Union Army.

■ Union blockade of southern ports begins.

■ The first *Confiscation Act* is passed allowing seizure of all "property" used for insurrection purposes, including slaves.

■ Detective **Allen Pinkerton** uncovers a plot to assassinate Lincoln, and forms a counterespionage organization that discourages General McClellan from action by exaggerating Confederate troop strength.

1862   ■ **Forts Henry** and **Donelson** are captured
        by Union troops under **General Ulysses S.
        Grant**, opening a major southern route.
        ■ New Orleans is captured.

        ■ **Battle of Shiloh**, the bloodiest battle of the
        war thus far, is fought, altering perceptions
        of a "short" war.

        • 13,000 Union dead; 11,000 Confederate
          dead.

        • The Union "wins."

        ■ The Confederacy is forced to adopt a draft.

        ■ McClellan attacks Virginia.

        • Led by **General Robert E. Lee**,
          Confederate troops hold off the Union
          forces.

        • Buoyed by this, **Jefferson Davis** orders
          his troops on the offensive.

        ■ *Second Confiscation Act* orders taking of
        property of all who support rebellion, even
        if that "support" is merely living in the
        south and paying taxes.

        ■ **Battle of Antietam** leads Lincoln to
        announce emancipation, on January 1,
        1863, of all slaves in states whose people
        "shall then be in rebellion against the
        United States."

1863   ■ *National Banking Act* leads to a uniform
        currency across the nation.
        ■ The Union adopts a draft.

- ■ Black soldiers are allowed to join the Union Army.
  - Many remain in service after the war and go west. The Indians call them **"Buffalo soldiers,"** as their dark skin and tenacity in battle are like fierce buffalo.
- ■ The blockade leads to food riots in many southern cities.
- ■ **Battle of Chancellorsville** (VA) is a surprise victory for the Confederacy over larger Union forces, thanks to the strategy of Lee and Jackson.
- ■ **Battle of Gettysburg** (PA) is disastrous for the Confederacy, and the turning point in the war.
  - Lee's strategy, which sees over 4,000 dead and 24,000 missing or wounded, is blamed.
- ■ **Vicksburg** (MS) surrenders.
- ■ Rioters in New York protest the draft.

1864
- ■ In the **Battle of Cold Harbor** (VA) Grant loses over 12,000 men in just a few hours, but vows to fight it out ". . . if it takes all summer."
- ■ **Lincoln** requests a Republican Party platform abolishing slavery nationwide for upcoming election.
- ■ Union **General William Tecumseh Sherman** enters Atlanta.
- ■ **Lincoln** is re-elected.

■ Jefferson Davis proposes Confederate emancipation.

■ Sherman's **March to the Sea** in Georgia decimates the countryside. His "scorched earth" policy of burning crops and property leaves nothing in its wake.

1865 ■ Sherman continues his drive through the Carolinas.

■ The *Thirteenth Amendment* **abolishes slavery.**

■ **Hampton Roads Conference** (VA) lays the groundwork for southern re-unification into the U.S.

■ General Robert E. Lee **surrenders** to General Ulysses S. Grant at the **Appomattox Courthouse** (VA).

■ **John Wilkes Booth** assassinates Lincoln at the performance of *Our American Cousin* at **Ford's Theatre.**

■ Jefferson Davis is captured, and remaining Confederate forces lay down their arms.

■ **The war ends**.

• The Union has lost 360,222 men; the Confederacy 258,000; with over 471,000 wounded on both sides.

Reconstruction
1865 – 1877

14

1865   ■ **President Andrew Johnson** starts **Reconstruction.**

■ Confederate leaders rise again.

■ ***Black Codes*** are enacted.

■ Congress refuses seating of southern delegates.

■ ***Thirteenth Amendment*** to the Constitution is ratified.
   • "Neither slavery nor involuntary servitude, except as a punishment for crime whereof the party shall have been duly convicted, shall exist within the United States or any place subject to their jurisdiction."

1866   ■ ***Fourteenth Amendment*** is passed, to apply Civil Rights, as guaranteed by the Bill of Rights, to all states. It is rejected by southern states.

1867   ■ ***Military Reconstruction Act*** is passed.
   ■ ***Tenure of Office Act*** is passed.

■ Southern states call a **Constitutional Convention.**

■ **Secretary of State W. H. Seward** purchases **Alaska**.

1868   ■ The nation is in turmoil:
- Impeachment/acquittal of Andrew Johnson
- Readmission of southern states

■ *Fourteenth Amendment* is ratified.

■ **Ulysses S. Grant** is elected president.

1870   ■ The *Fifteenth Amendment* bars denying voting rights *"on account of race, color, or previous condition of servitude."*

■ *Enforcement Act* is passed, making it a crime to interfere with voting rights.

1871   ■ *Ku Klux Klan Act* is passed.

■ Second *Enforcement Act* becomes law.

■ *Treaty of Washington,* designed to settle questions of Canada/U.S. border rights, claims against Britain for damage to the Confederate ship *Alabama,* and some North Atlantic fishing rights, is signed.

1872   ■ *Amnesty Act* is passed.

■ Debtors want **greenbacks** (paper money) to remain as legal currency. Established as legal tender in 1871.

■ Grant is elected to second term.

1873   ■ *Slaughterhouse Cases* in Louisiana raise issue of monopoly, but Supreme Court rules no violation of Thirteenth or Fourteenth Amendments.

■ **Panic of 1873** hits nationwide.

1874 ■ Grant refuses to increase paper money supply.
■ Democrats become House majority.
■ Congress makes gold sole monetary standard.

1875 ■ Corruption indictment of Grant appointees
■ Passage of new *Civil Rights Act*
■ Greenbacks to be converted to gold by 1878.

1876 ■ ***U.S. v. Reese:*** Constitution "does not guarantee right to vote."
■ ***U.S. v. Cruikshank:*** U.S. has no right to intervene in private discrimination.

1877 ■ Congress elects **Rutherford B. Hayes** president after disputes in general election lead many to believe **Samuel Tilden** is winner.
■ Black **"Exodusters"** migrate to Kansas.

15 The Shaping of a Nation

1857 – 1877

1857
- First publication of *Harper's* and *Atlantic Monthly.*
- New York and St. Louis are connected by rail.

1858
- **George M. Pullman** puts sleeping cars on trains.

1859
- **Dan D. Emmett**, who has never been to the South, writes *Dixie* for a minstrel show.

1860
- The **Pony Express** is started; ends when made unnecessary by the telegraph.
- The first "dime novels" are published.

1861
- **Yale** grants the country's first Ph.D.

1862
- The first enclosed baseball field opens in Brooklyn.

1863
- **Brotherhood of Railway Locomotive Engineers,** one of the earliest labor unions, is formed.

1864
- **"In God We Trust"** appears on U.S. coins.
- **Trade unionism** grows with organization of the cigar makers and iron molders.

1866   ■ Congress authorizes the coining of the nickel.

1868   ■ For federal employees, eight-hour workday becomes law.
        ■ Amnesty declared for all involved in Civil War.

1870   ■ **National Weather Bureau** is established.
        ■ **Senator Hiram R. Revels** is seated. First Black senator in U.S.

1871   ■ **Chicago fire** decimates much of the city.

1873   ■ Plagues of grasshoppers devastate western farmlands.

1874   ■ The first bridge to span the Mississippi River is opened.

1876   ■ The first **National League** baseball game is played.

1877   ■ **George B. Selden** makes two-cylinder "gas carriage."

16

West & South

1862 – 1896

1862   ■ *Homestead Act*
- Turns over 270 million acres (10 percent of U.S.) of public domain to private citizens.

■ *Morrill Land Grant Act*
- Creates agricultural and mechanical colleges in every state, plus 30,000 acres for these schools.
- One of the most important pieces of legislation in U.S. history.

1865   ■ *Thirteenth Amendment* is ratified.

1869   ■ **Union Pacific,** the first transcontinental railroad, is completed.

1874   ■ Barbed wire fence is patented, leading to the closing of "free" range.

1876   ■ **Battle of Little Big Horn** ("Custer's Last Stand")
- **Lt. Colonel George Armstrong Custer's** troops are decimated by Lakota and Cheyenne tribes.

1878   ■ *Timber and Stone Act*
         • Designates lands for their value (in timber and stone) at $2.50 per acre.

1880   ■ **1880-81:** Publication of major works on native tribes:
         • *Our Indian Wards* (Maypenney)
         • *A Century of Dishonor* (Jackson)

1882   ■ **1882-83:** Construction begins on **Santa Fe, Southern Pacific** and **Northern Pacific** railroads.

1883   ■ **Civil Rights** cases repeal most earlier civil rights legislation and *establish segregation as lawful.*
         ■ **National Time Zones** are established.

1887   ■ *Dawes Severalty Act*
         • Dissolution of community-owned native tribes' land
         • Allowance for individual native-tribe ownership of government-allotted land and citizenship
         ■ *Hatch Act* puts agricultural experimental stations in every state to expand technology.

1889   ■ **North** and **South Dakota, Washington** and **Montana** are granted statehood.

1890
- **Wounded Knee Massacre** results in killing of hundreds of Lakota during disarmament fiasco by U.S. Seventh Cavalry.
  - Considered the last "official" armed conflict of the "Indian Wars."
- **Wyoming** and **Idaho** gain statehood.
- **First National Park (Yosemite)** is established.
- Frontier is officially "closed" by announcement of Census Bureau.

1896
- *Plessy v. Ferguson:* Establishes concept of **"Separate but Equal"** facilities for Blacks and whites.
  - *Cummins v. County Board of Education* (1899) will establish that this applies to education.
- **Rural Free Delivery (RFD)** of mail is established.
- **Utah** gains statehood.

The Gilded Age
1873 – 1900

1873   ■ The end of silver dollar coinage

1876   ■ **Rutherford B. Hayes** is elected president amid controversy.

1877   ■ *Munn v. Illinois:* Railroads are "private property acting in the public good" and are thus subject to government regulation.

1878   ■ *Bland-Allison Act* requires the treasury to buy silver.
        ■ **Susan B. Anthony's** women's suffrage amendment is defeated.

1880   ■ **James A. Garfield** is elected president.

1881   ■ **Garfield** assassinated, **Chester A. Arthur** assumes presidency.

1883   ■ *Pendleton Civil Service Act* outlaws political contributions by office holders and establishes the **Civil Service Commission**.

1884   ■ U.S. enters a depression.
        ■ **Grover Cleveland** is elected president.

1886   ■ *Wabash, St. Louis, and Pacific Railroad Co. v. Illinois:*
- States cannot control interstate railroad lines.
- Only Congress can regulate interstate commerce rates.

1887   ■ **Interstate Commerce Commission** is formed.
■ Farm prices collapse.

1888   ■ **Benjamin Harrison** is elected president.

1890   ■ *McKinley Tariff* adds 4 percent to the cost of imported goods, allowing American businesses to undersell other countries and prosper.
■ *Sherman Silver Purchase Act* sets amount of silver government must buy by weight, not dollars.
■ *"The Mississippi Plan"* is inaugurated in the South to prevent Blacks (and poor whites) from voting, by establishing a poll tax with unreasonable requirements for payment.

1892   ■ **Populist** convention is held in Omaha (NE).
■ **Grover Cleveland** is elected president, and is the only president (to date) to serve two non-consecutive terms.

1893   ■ *Sherman Silver Purchase Act* is repealed.
■ U.S. enters another depression, which will last until 1897.

1894 ■ After Democrats cut virtually all **"McKinley"** tariffs, the *Wilson-Gorman Tariff* re-establishes them.

■ **Pullman Strike**
- 120,000 striking railroad workers virtually paralyze the nation.
- Cleveland calls in federal troops.
- **Eugene V. Debs**, president of the railway union, is arrested and, while in prison, formulates plans that will make him the leading **Socialist** leader in the U.S.

■ **"Coxey's Army":** Mass march on Washington led by **Jacob S. Coxey** demanding that the government provide money for the poor and unemployed.

1896 ■ **William McKinley** is elected president.

1897 ■ *Dingley Act* raises tariff rates still higher, but expands reciprocity.
■ *Maximum Freight Rate Case:* Supreme Court rules **Interstate Commerce Commission** does not have the power to set rates, weakening ICC.

1898 ■ The Louisiana **"grandfather clause"** establishes literacy and property qualifications for voting, but exempts sons and grandsons of those eligible to vote before 1867.

1900 ■ McKinley is re-elected.
■ *Gold Standard Act:* Paper money backed by gold.

18 Working Life & New Trends
1873 – 1915

1873   ■ **Stock market panic** rocks the nation.

1877   ■ **Railroad strikes** occur across the U.S.

1879   ■ *Progress and Poverty* by **Henry George** warns of the hard times that change brings. ■ **Thomas Alva Edison** invents the incandescent light bulb.

1881   ■ *Federal Trademark Law* is enacted.

1882   ■ **Standard Oil Trust** is formed.

1884   ■ **Mark Twain** writes *Huckleberry Finn,* hailed as the first true American novel.

1886   ■ **American Federation of Labor (AFL)** is founded.

1889   ■ Edison invents the motion-picture camera.

1890   ■ *Sherman Anti-Trust Act* is passed.

1892   ■ **Homestead Steel Strike** shakes up industry.

1895   ■ *U.S. v. E.C. Knight Co*. blunts Sherman Act.
- Manufacturing of almost all of a product is not *de facto* restraint of trade.
- If all manufacturing is done within one state, interstate laws do not apply.

1896   ■ *Holden v. Hardy:* Supreme Court upholds law limiting miners' work hours, citing dangers from fatigue due to nature of work.

1901   ■ **1901-03:** *U.S. Steel* and *Ford Motor Company* founded.

1903   ■ The first **World Series** is played, Boston v. Pittsburgh—Boston wins, 5 to 3.

1905   ■ *Lochner v. New York*
- Supreme Court voids law regulating bakers' work hours, as trade is "not dangerous enough" to warrant them.
- Law also restrains workers from selling their talents as they choose, thus violating Fourteenth Amendment.

■ **Industrial Workers of the World** ("Wobblies") is founded.

1908   ■ *Muller v. Oregon:* Supreme Court, in effect, voids *Lochner* as when it applies to women, ruling that their work must be regulated, as the health of women "becomes an object of public interest and care in order to preserve the strength and vigor of the race."

■ Ford introduces the Model T.

1911   ■ The electric self-starter for automobiles is invented.

■ **Triangle Shirtwaist Company Fire**
- 147 workers (mostly women) burn in "sweatshop" due to unsafe conditions.
- Public outcry strengthens unions' and workers' rights causes.

1913   ■ Ford introduces first moving assembly line.

■ **U.S. Department of Labor** is created.

■ The 60-story **Woolworth Building** opens; tallest structure of its day.

1915   ■ *Birth of a Nation,* first "feature length" story is filmed; directed by **D. W. Griffith.**

Empire Building
1866 – 1914

1866   ■ Transatlantic cable is completed.
       ■ France withdraws from Mexico.

1867   ■ U.S. acquires **Alaska** and **Midway**.

1868   ■ ***Burlingame Treaty*** is signed with China.

1870   ■ Annexation of Dominican Republic is rejected.

1878   ■ U.S. products dominate Paris World's Fair.

1883   ■ The "new Navy" is formed.

1887   ■ U.S. granted naval rights to **Pearl Harbor, Hawaii**.

1889   ■ **Pan-American Conference** is held in Washington, D.C.

1890   ■ **Captain Alfred T. Mahan** writes *The Influence of Sea Power upon History*, which has a worldwide influence on expansionist theory.

1893
- U.S. enters a serious depression.
- **Frederick Jackson Turner** expounds his **"Frontier"** thesis: The U.S. frontier was the essential building block of our character, so we should look to new frontiers, overseas.
- Revolution in Hawaii creates havoc.

1896
- The **Cuban Revolution** begins.
- **Sino-Japanese War** ends with Japan victorious.
- **William McKinley** is elected president.

1898
- Sinking of U.S. warship *Maine* leads to **Spanish-American War**.
- U.S. annexes **Hawaii** and **Wake Island**.

1899
- *Treaty of Paris* ends **Spanish-American War,** granting independence to Cuba and ceding the Philippines, Puerto Rico and Guam to U.S.
- **United Fruit Company** gives U.S. power in Central America.
- **"Open Door"** note is sent to European powers in China, urging free trade.
- **Philippine Insurrection** begins, led by Emilio Aguinaldo.

1900
- **U.S. exports** reach a record **$1.5 billion.**

1901
- **Theodore Roosevelt** becomes president after McKinley is assassinated.
- Aguinaldo is captured, ending Philippine Insurrection.

■ *Hay-Pauncefote Treaty:* Britain "steps aside" in U.S. **Panama Canal** plans.

1903 ■ Panama breaks from Colombia.
- A move instigated by Roosevelt and U.S. to eliminate Colombian demands concerning the Panama Canal.
- U.S. is granted canal rights in Panama.

■ *Platt Amendment,* forbidding Cuba from making treaties without U.S. approval, is forced into Cuban Constitution.

1904 ■ *The Roosevelt Corollary:* A latter-day "addendum" to the *Monroe Doctrine* that gives U.S. the right to step into any fray that threatens its sovereignty and makes it "an international police power."

1905 ■ *Taft-Katsura Agreement*
- U.S. grants Japan hegemony over Korea.
- Japan agrees not to undermine U.S. position in Philippines.

■ **Portsmouth Conference:** Roosevelt serves as mediator in Sino-Russian War.

■ U.S. imposes financial supervision over Dominican Republic.

1906 ■ Concern over heavy Asian immigration causes San Francisco to segregate Asian schoolchildren.
■ **U.S. invades Cuba** to quell a revolution and stays until 1909. Numerous other occupations will follow.

1907   ■ **"Great White Fleet"**
- U.S. Navy is sent on world tour to impress the Japanese with its power.
- Japan, heeding the warning, builds up its own fleet.

■**"Gentleman's Agreement"** with Japan unofficially reduces Asian immigration.

1908   ■ *Root-Takahira Agreement*
- U.S. recognizes Japan's interests in Manchuria (China).
- Japan pledges no interference with U.S. possessions in the Pacific.

1910   ■ **Mexican Revolution** begins.

1912   ■ U.S. troops re-enter Cuba and occupy Nicaragua under the Roosevelt Corollary.

1914   ■ U.S. troops invade Mexico.
■ **Panama Canal** opens.
■ **World War I** begins.

The
Progressive Era
1893 – 1920

1893 ■ **Anti-Saloon League** is founded. It will later join with the **Women's Christian Temperance Union** to crusade against alcohol consumption.

1895 ■ **Booker T. Washington's** *Atlanta Compromise* speech accepts **Separate but Equal** in race relations.

1898 ■ *Holden v. Hardy:* Supreme Court supports the use of State police powers to "protect health, safety, and morals."

1901 ■ **President McKinley** is assassinated. **Theodore Roosevelt** becomes president.

1904 ■ *Northern Securities Case:* Supreme Court orders dissolution of **J.P. Morgan's Northern Securities Company,** declaring it a trust harming the public.
■ **"Teddy" Roosevelt** is elected president.

1905 ■ **Niagara Falls Convention** meets in protest against *Atlanta Compromise* and pledges staunch militancy.

1906   ■ *Hepburn Act* imposes stricter control over railroads and vastly expands strength of ICC.
■ *Pure Food and Drug Act*
- Inspired by *The Jungle* by **Upton Sinclair**
- Beginnings of government inspection for purity and safety
- *Meat Inspection Act* is passed.

1907   ■ U.S. suffers an economic panic.

1908   ■ **William Howard Taft** is elected president.
■ *Muller v. Oregon:* Supreme Court upholds Oregon law limiting working hours for women, after future **Justice Louis Brandeis** provides extensive scientific data on the harmful effects of long hours of work.

1909   ■ **National Association for Advancement of Colored People (NAACP)** is founded.
■ *Payne-Aldrich Tariff:* After **Sereno E. Payne** introduces a bill to lower tariffs, protectionists led by **Senator Nelson W. Aldrich** restore many of the cuts thereby, in effect, assuring the status quo.

1910   ■ *Mann-Elkins Act*
- Increases ICC powers.
- Supports eight-hour workdays and mine safety.

■ *Mann Act*

- AKA: The *White Slave Traffic Act.*

- Prohibits interstate/international transportation of women for immoral purposes.

■ **Ballinger-Pinchot Controversy**

- **Secretary of the Interior Richard A. Ballinger** removes over 1 million acres of forest and mineral land from the reserved list.

- He fires **Gifford Pinchot** who questions sale of coal lands in Alaska.

1912 ■ **Theodore Roosevelt** runs for president on the **Progressive ("Bull Moose") Party** ticket, gaining the largest third-party vote (until **Ross Perot** in 1992 election).
■ **Woodrow Wilson** is elected president.

1913 ■ *Sixteenth Amendment*, legalizing a **Federal Income Tax,** is passed.
■ *Seventeenth Amendment,* providing for direct election of U.S. Senators, is passed.

■ *Underwood Tariff* drastically reduces or eliminates many tariffs.

■ *Federal Reserve Act* establishes a central banking system with 12 district banks to handle the reserves of nation's member banks.

1914 ■ *Federal Trade Commission Act*
- **FTC,** replacing the **Bureau of Corporations,** investigates unfair trade practices.

■ *Clayton Anti-Trust Act*
- Outlaws price discrimination and interlocking directorates.
- Extension of *Sherman Anti-Trust Act* of 1890.

■ **Margaret Sanger** is indicted for mailing "obscene literature" (advice on contraception). Many view her work as a threat to the family.

1916 ■ **Wilson** is re-elected.
■ *Federal Farm Loan Act*
- Brought about by concern for food shortages due to WWI.
- Creates 12 federally supported banks to lend money to farmers who belonged to credit institutions.

1919 ■ *Eighteenth Amendment* (prohibition) is ratified.

1920 ■ *Nineteenth Amendment* (women's suffrage) is ratified.
■ **Warren G. Harding** is elected president.
■ **Socialist** party candidate **Eugene V. Debs** gets 918,000 votes; he runs while in prison.

21

World War I
1914 – 1920*

* [Although the war ended in 1918, important events connected to it transpired through 1920.]

1914   ■ **World War I** begins in Europe.

1915   ■ Germany declares British Isles a "war zone."

        ■ German U-boats sink the *Lusitania* which carries 1,200 passengers, including 128 Americans.

        ■ **President Wilson** rejects entering the war.

        ■ **William Jennings Bryan** resigns as Secretary of State.

- Wants Wilson to warn Americans against travel because of potential "dangers."

- Wilson chooses, instead, to warn Germany against attacking ships with Americans aboard.

1916   ■ *Gore-McLemore Resolution* fails.

- Would prohibit Americans from travel on armed or contraband-carrying vessels.

- Wilson opposes this attack on his right to establish foreign policy and on American freedom of travel.

        ■ U.S. troops invade Mexico again.

■French ship *Sussex,* with four Americans aboard, attacked by German submarines.

■*National Defense Act* increases army and National Guard and establishes training camps.

■Running on the campaign slogan: "He Kept Us out of War," **Wilson** is re-elected.

1917 ■Germany declares "unrestricted submarine warfare."

■**Zimmerman telegram** urges Mexico to join Germany against the U.S., promising support for regaining lands lost to U. S.

■Revolution in Russia brings Communists to power.

■U.S. officially enters **WWI.**

■*Selective Service Act* (draft) is passed.

■*Espionage Act* is passed, forbidding "false statements" impeding the draft or promoting military insubordination.

■Race riot in East St. Louis (IL) as whites protest hiring of Blacks in defense plants.

■**War Industries Board** created to coordinate national economy and satisfy both war and domestic needs.

■*War Revenue Act* is passed with steeply graduated personal income tax, corporate income tax, excess profits tax, increased excise taxes on alcohol, tobacco, luxury items.

1918   ■ **Wilson** enumerates his *Fourteen Points,* which will provide a basis for the **League of Nations**.

■ *Sedition Act* is passed.

■ U.S troops enter Chateau-Thierry, France.

■ U.S. troops enter Russia.

■ Flu epidemic kills thousands.

■ Republicans win majority in congressional elections.

■ Armistice is declared.

1919   ■ **Paris Peace Conference** is held at Versailles, where Germany accepts blame for starting war.

   • Forced to give up Alsace-Lorraine and all other colonies, and ordered to pay $15 billion in reparations.

   • Because German people have not seen allied might on their own shores, **Adolf Hitler** will later exploit the agreement as "a betrayal … not a defeat," setting stage for WWII.

■ "May Day Bombs" add impetus to "Red Scare."

■ **American Legion** is founded to promote patriotism and defeat communism.

■ Race riot in Chicago called "The Red Summer."

■ Founding of the **U.S. Communist Party**.

■ Wilson suffers stroke.

- Rumors spread that his wife, Edith, is running the White House.

- **Vice President Thomas R. Marshall** ("What this country needs is a good five cent cigar") does not take over because no provision exists for declaring a president unable to perform his duties.

■ Senate rejects *Treaty of Paris,* removing U.S. as a power in Europe and, subsequently, in League of Nations.

■ *Schenk v. U.S.*

- Supreme Court upholds abridgement of First Amendment rights in time of war.

- "...fire in a crowded theater."

1920   ■ **Attorney General A. Mitchell Palmer,** to protect U.S. from Communists, stages raids in 33 cities without search warrants.

- Arrests thousands, holding them without bail or counsel.

- Approximately 600 will be deported. All others will be released.

■ *Nineteenth Amendment* is ratified; women have the vote.

The "Twenties" Roar

1919 – 1929

1919 ■ *Eighteenth Amendment* (prohibition) is ratified.

1920 ■ *Nineteenth Amendment* (women's suffrage) is ratified.
■ **Warren G. Harding** is elected president.
■ First commercial radio broadcast is heard.

1921 ■ *Federal Highway Act* provides aid for state roads.
■ Immigration quotas are established.
■ **Sacco** and **Vanzetti** are convicted and sentenced to death.
■ *Sheppard-Towner Act* funds state pediatric and maternity clinics, demonstrating strength of women's lobby.

1922 ■ Economic recovery from the war starts out strong.

1923 ■ **Harding** dies; **Calvin Coolidge** becomes president.
■ **Ku Klux Klan** activity reaches all-time high.
■ An **Equal Rights for Women** amendment is demanded.

1924   ■ **Teapot Dome** scandal exposes corruption in Harding administration.

       ■ *National Origins Act* strictly sets quotas on immigration based on population as of 1867 (later revised to 1920).

       ■ **Calvin Coolidge** is elected President.

1925   ■ *Scopes Trial* pits Clarence Darrow against William Jennings Bryan.

1927   ■ **Sacco** and **Vanzetti** executed amid much protest.

       ■ **Lindbergh** flies solo across the Atlantic.

       ■ **Babe Ruth** hits 60 home runs in a season.

       ■ *The Jazz Singer* popularizes sound in the movies, creating craze for the "talkies."

1928   ■ Stock market soars to new heights.

       ■ **Herbert Hoover** is elected president.

1929   ■ Stock market plummets.

       ■ The **Great Depression** begins.

23

Meanwhile in the World

1922 – 1941

1922   ■ **Benito Mussolini** rises to power in Italy.

1924   ■ *Dawes's German Reparations Plan* reduces Germany's annual payments and extends payback period.
      ■ U.S. leaves Dominican Republic.

1926   ■ American troops occupy Nicaragua.

1928   ■ *Kellogg-Briand Pact,* signed by 62 nations, condemns the use of war as "an instrument of national policy."

1929   ■ *Young Plan* reduces German reparations still further, but it is too late; German economy is in shambles.

1930   ■ *Hawley-Smoot Tariff* raises rates still higher.

1931   ■ Japan marches into Manchuria.

1932   ■ **Secretary of State Henry Stimson** declares U.S. will not recognize impairment of Chinese sovereignty or "Open Door" policy.
      ■ **Franklin D. Roosevelt (FDR)** is elected president.

1933   ■ **Adolf Hitler** rises to power in Germany.
        ■ U.S. recognizes Soviet Russia.
        ■ *Good Neighbor Policy* is established.

1934   ■ **Juan Batista** rises to power in Cuba.
        ■ *Reciprocal Trade Agreements Act* is passed allowing president to reduce tariffs as much as 50 percent to "most favored nations."

1935   ■ Italy invades Ethiopia.
        ■ *Neutrality Act* is passed prohibiting arms shipments to either side once the president has determined a "belligerency" exists.

1936   ■ U.S. votes for nonintervention at **Pan-American Conference**.
        ■ **Civil War** breaks out in **Spain.**
        ■ *Second Neutrality Act* is passed forbidding loans to belligerents.

1937   ■ *Third Neutrality Act:* "Cash and Carry" concept states that all foreign purchases must be paid for in full at time of receipt.
        ■ **China Incident**
        • Japan "accidentally" sinks the naval ship *Panay.*
        • FDR demands and gets an apology.
        • FDR calls on nations to "quarantine" Japan, calling the country an example of "world lawlessness."

1938 ■ Mexico nationalizes U.S.-owned oil companies.

■ **Munich Conference** is held. British **Prime Minister Neville Chamberlain** returns with assurances from Hitler that there will be "peace in our time."

1939 ■ *Nazi-Soviet Pact* is signed.

■ Germany invades Poland.

■ **World War II** begins.

■ U.S. repeals arms embargo to allies.

1940 ■ Soviets invade Finland.

■ **Committee to Defend America by Aiding the Allies** is formed.

■ **America First Committee**, an isolationist group led by **Charles Lindbergh**, is formed.

■ *Selective Service and Training Act* is passed.

• First "peace-time" draft in U.S.

• FDR pledges he "will not send American boys to fight a foreign war."

1941 ■ *Lend-Lease Act* allows U.S. to furnish supplies to the Allies.

■ Germany attacks the Soviet Union.

■ U.S. freezes Japanese assets under its control.

■ **FDR** and **Churchill** issue *Atlantic Charter.*

■ *Greer* **Incident:**

- Germany fires on an American destroyer, *USS Greer,* rousing U.S. ire.
- No mention is made of the fact that the destroyer was tailing the vessel and reporting its position to Allied forces.

■ **Japan** attacks **Pearl Harbor (HI).**

■ **U.S.** enters **World War II.**

The New Deal

1931 – 1941

1931
- ***Scottsboro Case:*** nine Black men are falsely charged with raping two white women; the men are imprisoned.
- Hoover declares moratorium on repayment of WWI debts and reparations to retard collapse of international monetary system.

1932
- **Reconstruction Finance Corporation** provides loans to banks, insurance companies, railroads, state and local governments.
- 15,000 WWI veterans come to Washington to demand bonuses promised by government but not due to be paid until 1945.
  - After being refused, many set up camp in D.C.
  - **General Douglas MacArthur** disperses them with military force.
- **Franklin Delano Roosevelt (FDR)** is elected president.
  - Promising a **"New Deal for America,"** he defeats Hoover.

1933
- Unemployment in U.S. reaches 13 million.
- FDR orders national "Bank Holiday" to halt all transactions.

■ *Agricultural Adjustment Act* (**AAA**) is passed to control overproduction and pay farmers for losses.

■ **Tennessee Valley Authority** (**TVA**) is established.

■ *National Industrial Recovery Act* (**NIRA**) is passed, which sets nationwide standards for business administration.

- Establishes the **National Recovery Administration** (**NRA**) to meet with competing businesses and establish fair trade practices.

- Ensures unions the right to collective bargaining.

■ *Twentieth* ("Lame Duck") *Amendment* is ratified, moving presidential inaugurations from March 4 to January 20.

■ *Twenty-First Amendment* (prohibition repeal) is ratified.

1934   ■ **Dr. Francis E. Townsend** proposes the *Old Age Revolving Pension Plan,* which states that the government must give each citizen over age 60 a monthly stipend of $200, which must be spent within that month.

■ **Huey Long** forms the "Share Our Wealth Society," urging seizure of all income over $1 million and inheritances over $5 million to provide homesteads and income for the poor.

■ *Wheeler Howard Act* ("Indian Reorganization") is passed, restoring native lands to tribal ownership and forbidding further division of land into individual parcels.

■ Democrats win overwhelming congressional victories.

■ **Father Francis Coughlin**, an anti-Communist, anti-capitalist, anti-Semitic radio preacher with a huge audience, organizes the **National Union for Social Justice** to combat the New Deal.

1935 ■ *Emergency Relief Appropriation Act* authorizes president to provide public works programs for the unemployed.
- **Works Progress Administration (WPA)**
- **Resettlement Administration (RA)**
- **Rural Electrification Administration (REA)**
- **National Youth Administration (NYA)**

■ *Schechter Poultry Corporation v. U.S.* invalidates the **NIRA** as unconstitutional.

■ *National Labor Relations* (Wagner) *Act* is passed, granting workers right to organize and bargain collectively.
- Establishes the **Labor Relations Board** to ensure democratic union elections and eradicate unfair labor practices.

■ *Social Security Act* is passed.

■ Huey Long is assassinated.

■ **Committee for Industrial Organization (CIO)** is established.

1936   ■ *U.S. v. Butler* invalidates the **AAA.**
        ■ FDR defeats **Alf Landon** for a second term.

1937   ■ **United Auto Worker's** union organizes a series of "sit-down" strikes. Workers stay on the job, but refuse to work.
        ■ FDR frustrated by Supreme Court rulings, threatens "court packing," which would forcibly retire justices over age 70 and allow him to name up to six new ones. The plan fails, but the Court does begin a somewhat more lenient review of New Deal policies.
        ■ *NLRB v. Jones & Laughlin* upholds the *Wagner Act.*
        ■ **Memorial Day Massacre:** Chicago police open fire on striking steelworkers and others who are peacefully picketing.
        ■ **Farm Security Administration** is established to aid migratory farm workers.

1938   ■ **AFL** expels all **CIO** unions.
        ■ *Fair Labor Standards Act* is passed.
        • Forbids child labor
        • Establishes minimum wage
        • Establishes 40-hour week in many areas
        ■ Unemployment drops to 10.4 million.
        ■ The first **XEROX** image is created.

1939 ■ **Black** opera singer **Marian Anderson** gives Lincoln Memorial concert.
- She had been refused the right to perform in a hall owned by the **Daughters of the American Revolution (DAR)**.
- **First Lady Eleanor Roosevelt** arranges this "alternate" concert.

■ Nylon is introduced commercially.

1940 ■ FDR defeats **Wendell Wilkie**, becoming the first (and only) president elected to a third term.

1941 ■ **March on Washington Movement:** All-Black organization threatens to take its grievances (jobs, equal rights, etc.) to the streets.

■ FDR establishes the **Fair Employment Practices Committee**, which forbids discrimination in war industries and government.

■ U.S. Ambassador to Japan, **Joseph Grew**, warns of potential surprise attack on U.S.

■ FDR amends *Neutrality Act* to allow merchant ships to be armed.

World War II
1941 – 1945

1941 ■ **Japan** attacks **Pearl Harbor (HI)** on Sunday, December 7.

1942 ■ **National War Labor Board** and **War Production Board** are established.

■ Over 100,000 Japanese-Americans are interned.

■ **War Manpower Commission** is established.

■ **Bataan "Death March"** in the Philippines inflames U.S. hatred even more.

■ **Coral Sea** and **Midway naval battles** bolster morale.

■ **Office of War Information (OWI)** is established.

■ **Manhattan** (A-Bomb) **Project** is begun.

■ **Allies** invade **North Africa.**

■ **Republicans** win major gains in **Congress.**

■ Production of synthetic rubber begins.

1943 ■ Russians defeat Germans at Stalingrad.

■ Soft coal and anthracite miners go on strike in U.S.

■ **Office of War Mobilization** is established.

■ *Smith-Connally War Labor Disputes Act* passed.

- President may seize any strike-bound company deemed to be in the national interest.

- 30-day "cooling off" period before striking is required.

■ Race riots tear up Detroit, the Harlem section of New York City, and 45 other cities.

■ Allies land in Italy, which soon surrenders.

■ **Teheran Conference** is held.

- Stalin, Churchill and FDR agree to "second front."

- **Operation Overlord** (Invasion of Normandy) is started.

1944 ■ FDR *Economic Bill of Rights* proposes:
- Decent jobs

- Food/shelter/clothing commitment

- Financial security during unemployment, illness or old age

■ The **War Refugee Board** is established.

■ The Supreme Court upholds the legality of Japanese-American internments.

■ *GI Bill of Rights* is passed, which offers the benefit of free college education for returning GI's.

■ **D-Day, June 6:** Allies invade Western Europe.

- **Dumbarton Oaks Conference** sets the stage for **United Nations** formation.
- FDR is re-elected to a fourth term, although he is obviously quite ill.
- U.S. retakes the Philippines.

1945
- **Yalta Conference,** under heavy secrecy, makes plans for post-war division of conquered European and Asian countries.
- Allied victories at **Iwo Jima** and **Okinawa.**
- **FDR** dies; **Truman** becomes president.
- The **United Nations** is founded.
- **Germany surrenders.**
- **Potsdam Conference** achieves agreement on the handling of post-war Germany amidst deteriorating relations.
- **A-Bomb** tested at Alamogordo (NM).
- Truman orders A-bomb attacks on **Hiroshima** and **Nagasaki.**
- **Japan surrenders.**

Post-War to JFK

1945 – 1960

1945   ■ *Truman's 21 Points* economic message urges extension of unemployment benefits, increase in minimum wage, permanent farm price supports, new public works projects and much of FDR's *Economic Bill of Rights.*

1946   ■ **Iran Crisis:** Russia refuses to leave until U.S. promises oil concessions.

■ The *Employment Act of 1946* promises that the Government will use its resources—including deficit spending, if needed—to assure "maximum employment, production and purchasing power."

■ The **"baby boom"** begins.

■ The *Baruch Plan* agrees to share U.S. nuclear information after the power is placed under an international agency.

■ **Secretary of State Henry A. Wallace** is fired for disagreeing with Truman's "get tough" policy with Soviets.

■ Inflation reaches 18.2 percent.

■ **Republicans** win both houses of **Congress.**

1947   ■ The *Truman Doctrine* announces U.S. intention to support any peoples resisting "subjugation . . . or outside pressures."

■ **Truman** orders investigation of "loyalty" of 3 million government employees and fires many "security risks."

■ Communists take over Hungary.

■ The *Taft-Hartley Act* is passed prohibiting "closed" (i.e., union members only) shops and allowing state's "right-to-work" laws.

■ The (General George) *Marshall Plan* to bring assistance to war-torn countries is announced.

■ **President's Committee on Civil Rights** issues *To Secure These Rights,* the blueprint for civil rights activism for the next two decades.

■ *National Security Act* is passed.

■ The *Rio Pact,* military alliance with Latin America, is signed.

1948   ■ Communists take over Czechoslovakia.
        ■ State of Israel is founded.

        ■ Soviets blockade Berlin. U.S. airlifts supplies.

        ■ **Truman** elected president to the surprise of many.

1949   ■ **NATO** is founded.
        ■ Russia explodes A-bomb.

        ■ Communists take over China.

1950 ■ **Klaus Fuchs** arrested as "atomic" spy.
■ Former Communist **Whittaker Chambers** accuses **Alger Hiss** of party membership.

- Hiss sues Chambers for slander and loses.
- Hiss found guilty of perjury and imprisoned.

■ **Senator Joseph A. McCarthy** alleges hundreds of communists in U.S. government.

■ U.S. announces a **Hydrogen Bomb Project.**

■ *NSC-68* is issued by **National Security Council** urging massive security buildups, in light of continuing Communist threat.

■ (Communist) North Korea invades (Democratic) South Korea and **Korean War** begins.

■ **Julius** and **Ethel Rosenberg** are arrested as "atomic" spies.

■ Marines land at Inchon (Korea).

■ The *McCarran Act* (Internal Security) requires members of "Communist front" organizations to register with government.

■ U.S. troops cross 38th parallel and enter North Korea.

■ China enters the war on North Korea's side.

1951   ■ Armistice talks begin in Korea.

■ *Dennis et al. v. U.S.:* Supreme Court upholds the conviction and imprisonment of 11 Communist leaders.

1952   ■ First hydrogen bomb is exploded.

■ **Dwight D. Eisenhower**, promising to "go to Korea" and end war if elected, handily defeats **Adlai Stevenson** for presidency.

■ Republicans also win both houses of Congress.

■ **Norman Vincent Peale** inspires America with the *Power of Positive Thinking*.

■ **Ralph Ellison** awakens America with the *Invisible Man.*

1953   ■ **Korean War ends:** At no time was it ever officially a "war"; it was always referred to as a "police action."

■ Josef Stalin dies.

■ Convicted atomic spies **Julius** & **Ethel Rosenberg** are executed.

■ **Robert A. Oppenheimer**, one of the creators of the atom bomb, is called a security risk.

■ *Termination Policy* calls for the liquidation of Indian reservations and an end to federal services.

■ U.S. enters an economic recession.

1954   ■ The **U.S. Air Force Academy** is founded.

■ General Motors manufactures the first Corvette.

■ St. Lawrence Seaway project inaugurated.

- ■ ***Brown v. Board of Education of Topeka:*** Supreme Court rules "Separate but Equal" education is not equal.

- ■ **CIA** intervenes in **Guatemala** and arms the rebels.

- ■ China attacks islands of Quemoy and Matsu where Nationalists have fled, while U.S. threatens massive, possibly nuclear, retaliation.

- ■ Senate condemns **Joseph McCarthy**.

1955

- ■ A civil war in South Vietnam brings **Ngo Dinh Diem** to power as president.
- ■ **AFL** and **CIO** merge.

- ■ **Bandung Conference** calls for Third World countries to maintain neutrality.

- ■ **Rosa Parks** refuses to ride in the back of a bus in Montgomery (AL).

- ■ **Dr. Jonas Salk's** polio vaccine is approved.

1956

- ■ **Reverend Martin Luther King** organizes a bus boycott in Montgomery (AL).
- ■ ***Highway Act*** authorizes building of a 41,000-mile interstate highway system.

- ■ Soviets take Hungary.

- ■ **Eisenhower** is re-elected.

1957

- ■ The first ***Civil Rights Bill*** since the Civil War is enacted.
- ■ ***Eisenhower Doctrine*** promises U.S. intervention on behalf of any Middle East state threatened with Communist takeover.

■ Troops sent to enforce school desegregation in **Little Rock** (AR).

■ *Civil Rights Act* creates the **U.S. Commission on Civil Rights.**

■ **Soviet Union** launches **Sputnik**.

■ Another recession hits.

■ **4.3 million births** signal the peak of the "baby boom."

1958   ■ First Boeing 707 goes into service.
        ■ First U.S. satellite is launched.

■ U.S. intervenes in Lebanon.

■ **National Aeronautics & Space Administration (NASA)** is established.

■ Trouble flares anew in Quemoy and Matsu.

■ *National Defense Education Act* provides funding for upgrading education in science, mathematics and foreign languages.

■ **Soviet Premier Nikita Kruschev** declares that East Germany will control all of Berlin; he later backs off.

1959   ■ The world's first fully transistorized computer, the **RCA 501**, is introduced.
        ■ **Fidel Castro** takes power in **Cuba**.

1960   ■ After a coup against President Diem is defeated in South Vietnam, a dissident group called the **Vietcong** is formed.
        ■ **Francis Gary Power's** U.S. spy plane is downed over the USSR.

- **President Eisenhower** leaves office warning against "the Military-Industrial Complex" working to maintain high levels of defense spending at the expense of other goals.

- Greensboro (NC) becomes the site of the first **Equal Rights "sit-in."**

- **Student Nonviolent Coordinating Committee (SNCC)** for Civil Rights is formed.

- **John F. Kennedy (JFK)** defeats Richard M. Nixon for the presidency.

- Yet another recession is entered.

- GNP hits **$503.7 billion.**

The Vietnam Era
1961 – 1975

1961
- **Peace Corps** is founded by JFK.
- Miami-based Cuban refugees invade the **Bay of Pigs.**
- The **Berlin Wall** goes up.
- **"Freedom Riders"** head to the U.S. South in Civil Rights effort.

1962
- **Cuban Missile Crisis** threatens nuclear war between U.S. and Soviet Union.
- **John Glenn** orbits Earth.

1963
- **Martin Luther King** leads a Civil Rights March in D.C.
- U.S./Soviets sign limited nuclear test ban treaty.
- **Ngo Dinh Diem** is assassinated in Vietnam.
- **JFK** is assassinated; **Lyndon Baines Johnson (LBJ)** becomes president.
- **Betty Friedan** writes *The Feminine Mystique.*

1964   ■ **"Gulf of Tonkin"** incident grants Johnson exceptional powers in Vietnam.

■ *Civil Rights Act* is passed.

■ **"Free Speech"** movement begins on college campuses.

■ LBJ is elected president.

1965   ■ **Malcolm X** is assassinated.

■ The *Voting Rights Act of 1965* is enacted.

■ Race riot ignites **Watts** section of Los Angeles.

■ Anti-war "teach-ins" begin.

1966   ■ **National Organization for Women (NOW)** is formed.

■ *Miranda Act* upholds right of the arrested to be informed of their constitutional rights.

1967   ■ **Race riots** erupt in Newark, Detroit and many other cities.

■ **Peace rallies** are staged throughout U.S.

■ Israel wins **Six Day War** in the Middle East.

1968   ■ The **Tet Offensive** changes perception of Vietnam.

■ The **My Lai Massacre** is exposed.

■ Vietnam peace talks begin in Paris.

■ **Martin Luther King** is assassinated.

■ The *Civil Rights Act of 1968* is passed.

■ **Robert F. Kennedy** is assassinated.

- **Democratic National Convention** in Chicago leads to violence.
- **Richard M. Nixon** is elected president.

1969
- There are over 540,000 U.S. troops in Vietnam.
- The Stonewall Riot marks the beginning of **"Gay Pride"** movement.
- *Apollo 11* lands on the **moon.**
- Woodstock Festival of Peace and Love is held.
- **Nixon** begins withdrawal of U.S. troops from Vietnam.
- *Nixon Doctrine:* U.S. will help those nations that help themselves.
- U.S. policy of detente with the Soviet Union is announced.

1970
- U.S. invades Cambodia in pursuit of enemies.
- Student protesters are killed at **Kent** and **Jackson State** universities.
- **GNP** is at **$977.1 billion.**
- Suburbs surpass cities in population.

1971
- **Dr. Daniel Ellsberg** makes public *The Pentagon Papers.*
- *26th Amendment* (citizens age 18 and older can vote) is ratified.

1972   ■ **Nixon** visits China.

■ *SALT-I Treaty* on arms control is signed.

■ *Equal Rights Amendment* (**ERA**) is approved in Congress.

■ Democratic Committee HQ at the **Watergate Hotel** is broken into.

- **James McCord** and a team of Cuban "burglars" are caught and implicate **Howard Hunt** as their leader.

- Hunt has indirect ties to the White House as a consultant to **Special Counsel Charles Colson**.

- **Watergate** scandal begins.

- Despite some outrage in the press, Nixon denies any White House involvement and calls the matter a "second-rate burglary."

■ **Nixon** is re-elected.

■ A report in the *Washington Post* reveals that a check signed by Howard Hunt was found on one of the Cuban Watergate burglars. Reporters **Bob Woodward** and **Carl Bernstein** write the story.

1973   ■ *Roe v. Wade* establishes abortion as a legal option for women.

■ Cease-fire agreement reached in Vietnam.

■ An Arab oil embargo leads to shortages and rampant inflation.

■ **Vice President Spiro T. Agnew** resigns after pleading "no-contest" to income-tax evasion charges, and is replaced by **Gerald R. Ford**.

■ As more and more information appears to link high officials in the Nixon administration to Watergate, a **Select Committee on Presidential Campaign Activities** is voted by the Senate, under **Senator Sam Ervin.**

- The hearings will last into 1974 and, ultimately, expose direct evidence of the involvement of the president and his highest advisers in a series of questionable legal and extra-governmental activities.

- **Nixon** will attempt to stave off any findings by firing, or having fired, many of the prosecutors and investigators on the case in the so-called **"Saturday Night Massacre."**

- This backfires when public outrage is raised to unstoppable levels.

■ Richard Nixon announces to the nation, "I am not a crook."

1974   ■ A federal grand jury indicts Nixon's top officials.

- **John Mitchell** (Attorney General), **H.R. Haldeman** (Chief of Staff), **John Ehrlichman** (White House Aide), **Charles Colson** (Special Counsel), and others for conspiracy.

- Richard Nixon is named as an "unindicted co-conspirator."

■ The **House Judiciary Committee,** under **Congressman Peter Rodino,** approves three *Articles of Impeachment* with large bi-partisan support.

- *Article I* (27–11), *Article II* (28–10) (**Note:** *Numbers in parentheses indicate specific sections and lines within the articles.*)

- *Article II,* alleging "systematic abuse of power and violations of citizens' constitutional rights," is widely considered the most important.

- The Judiciary Committee also refuses approval on an article alleging income-tax fraud by Nixon as "personal" and, therefore, outside of the scope of an impeachable offense.

■ As Judiciary prepares to send the articles to the full House of Representatives for a vote, **Nixon** resigns and **Vice President Gerald R. Ford** becomes president.

1975   ■ Tentative Peace agreement between Egypt and Israel is reached.

■ **Vietnam War** ends.

28

The
Carter Years
1976 – 1981

1976   ■ *Hyde Amendment* refuses government funds for abortions.
       ■ **James Earl Carter** is elected president.

1977   ■ Carter announces U.S. policy on Human Rights.

1978   ■ *Bakke v. U of C* decision upholds affirmative action.
       ■ The *Panama Canal Treaties* are signed.
       ■ The *Camp David Accords* create peace between Egypt and Israel.
       ■ California voters approve *Proposition 13* to limit taxation.
       ■ Religious cult led by **Jim Jones** commits mass suicide in Guyana.

1979   ■ "Accident" at nuclear plant on **Three Mile Island** (PA)
       ■ Peace treaty between Egypt and Israel is signed.
       ■ The **"Moral Majority"** is formed.
       ■ The **Federal Reserve Board** begins "Tight Money" policy.

■ **Iranian terrorists** take over **American Embassy** and hold hostages.

■ *SALT II Treaty* is signed.

1980   ■ The Soviet Union invades Afghanistan.

■ U.S. orders grain embargo and boycotts Olympics in protest.

■ U.S. enters economic recession.

■ **Secretary of State Cyrus T. Vance** resigns over Carter foreign policy.

■ U.S. begins deregulation of oil prices and transportation industries.

■ **Ronald W. Reagan** is elected president.

1981   ■ Within days of Reagan's election, Iran hostages are freed.

29 The Reagan–Bush Years

1981 – 1992

1981 ■ First **AIDS** cases are reported.
■ **Reagan's** budget cuts approved by Congress.

■ *Economic Recovery Tax Act* is passed.

■ Soviets crack down on Polish activism. **Lech Walesa** is imprisoned.

■ U.S. increases role in El Salvador civil war.

■ **CIA** begins to train **Contras** in Nicaragua.

1982 ■ Prime rate drops to 14 percent.
■ **Strategic Arms Reduction Talks (START)** negotiations begin.

■ U.S. troops sent to Lebanon as "peacekeepers."

■ Unemployment hits 10.1 percent.

1983 ■ **Reagan** announces the **Strategic Defense Initiative ("Star Wars")**.
■ Unemployment is up to 10.2 percent

■ Over 50 percent of all women over 20 hold outside jobs.

■ **ERA** fails to achieve ratification.

■ Terrorists kill Marines in Lebanon.

■ **Reagan** orders invasion of the tiny island of **Grenada** because of claims that Cubans are using it as a military base.

- U.S. deploys missiles in Western Europe.
- The Contradora peace plan is proposed for Central America.

1984
- U.S. troops pull out of Lebanon.
- The CIA mines Nicaraguan harbors.
- Unemployment drops to 7.1 percent.
- **Reagan** is re-elected.

1985
- **Mikhail Gorbachev** rises to power in Soviet Union, declaring new policies of *Glasnost* and *Perestroika.*
- U.S. orders economic embargo against Nicaragua.

1986
- U.S. bombs Libya.
- *Tax Reform Act* closes some loopholes and removes 6 million poor from the tax rolls.
- The *Immigration Reform and Control Act* provides amnesty to undocumented aliens in U.S. prior to 1982.
- Republicans lose control of the Senate.
- **Iran-Contra** scandal (arms for hostages) breaks.

1987
- Summit is held in Washington, D.C. between Gorbachev and Reagan.
- **"Black Monday":** Stock market drops 508 points in one day.
- **Third World debt** hits **$1.2 trillion.**
- **U.S. trade deficit** hits **$170 million.**

1988   ■ Palestinians rise up on Israeli West Bank.

■ U.S. and Canada sign *Free Trade Agreement.*

■ Soviets agree to withdraw from Afghanistan.

■ Summit meeting is held in Moscow.

■ *INF* (Intermediate-range Nuclear Forces) *Treaty* signed.

■ U.S. warship shoots down Iranian airliner.

■ **AIDS awareness** increases as *Understanding AIDS* is mailed to 107 million U.S. households.

■ **George H. W. Bush** is elected president.

■ Terrorist bomb explodes in a Pan American airliner over Lockerbee, Scotland.

1989   ■ **Oliver North** is convicted in Iran-Contra trial.

■ Unemployment at 5.3 percent.

■ **Bush budget** tops **$1.16 trillion** with projected **deficit** of **$92 billion.**

■ *Exxon Valdez* spills 1,260,000 gallons of oil in Alaska.

■ Bush and Gorbachev meet in Malta.

■ Panama names **Manuel Noriega** head of government as National Assembly declares a "state of war" between Panama and U.S.

■ Bush sends 12,000 troops to invade Panama and capture Noriega.

1990   ■ Noriega surrenders to U.S. authorities and is imprisoned in Florida.

■ In South Africa, **Nelson Mandela** is freed after 27 years in prison.

■ Saddam Hussein sends tanks into Kuwait. Bush sends troops to Saudi Arabia.

■ U.N. and U.S. set January 15 deadline for Iraq to pull out of Kuwait.

1991 ■ After days of air strikes, the **Gulf** (ground) **War** begins and ends within 100 hours.

■ Unemployment at 6.1 percent.

■ New **budget** is **$1,446 billion. Deficit** is **$280.9 billion.**

■ **Rodney King** is beaten by police in Los Angeles; it is recorded on videotape.

■ **Mikhail Gorbachev** resigns as leader of the Soviet Union, which had effectively ceased to exist months before.

• The **Cold War** is over.

• **Berlin Wall** comes down.

1992 ■ Projected budget **deficit** hits **$352 billion.**

■ **H. Ross Perot** enters presidential race as Independent candidate and achieves the highest "third party" vote in history.

■ Jury **acquits police** in **Rodney King** beating, causing **race riots** in Los Angeles.

• Officers later tried and convicted of civil rights violations.

■ **William J. Clinton** is elected president with 43 percent of vote.

The Clinton Years

1993 – 2000

1993
- ◼ **World Trade Center** is bombed.
- ◼ **President Clinton** passes *Family and Medical Leave Act* **(FMLA).**
- ◼ White House aide **Vincent Foster** commits suicide.
- ◼ **Janet Reno** becomes first female **Attorney General.**
- ◼ Israel and PLO sign peace accord.
- ◼ **Russian Premier Boris Yeltsin** puts down Bloody Rebellion in Moscow and solidifies New Order.
- ◼ Civil War erupts in former Yugoslavian states of Bosnia and Herzegovina.
- ◼ Clinton's "Don't ask/Don't tell" rule allows gays in military.
- ◼ *North American Free Trade Agreement* **(NAFTA)** is passed.
- ◼ Peace pact signed between Britain and Northern Ireland.

1994
- ◼ **Republicans,** led by **Newt Gingrich** and guided by "Contract with America," gain **control** of **House** and **Senate** for first time in 40 years.
- ◼ Trade embargo with Vietnam is lifted.

■**CIA Agent Aldrick Ames** named as spy for Soviet Union.

■**Nelson Mandela** becomes first Black president of South Africa.

■**Paula Jones** files a civil lawsuit against President Clinton charging "sexual harassment" based on an alleged incident from 1991 when he was Governor of Arkansas.

- The president's attorneys argue for a stay of the suit until the president is out of office.

- U.S. Supreme Court, in 1997, rules unanimously that it can go forward, essentially saying the president is not above the law, and a minor civil suit will not have any major effect on the president's ability to run the country.

■**Richard Nixon** dies.

1995   ■U.N. peacekeeping forces come to Bosnia-Herzegovina.

■**O.J. Simpson** found not guilty of double homicide.

■Senate opens *"Whitewater"* hearings centered on questions of Vince Foster suicide and possible economic problems concerning the Clintons.

■Pat Buchanan, Malcolm "Steve" Forbes, Jr., and House Speaker Robert Dole run for Republican nomination for president.

■ **Alfred P. Murrah Building (OK)** is decimated by bomb, killing 168, including 18 children.

- **Timothy McVeigh** and **Terry Nichols** charged with bombing.

■ **"Unabomber"** claims 16th victim.

■ Federal government "shut down" in budget hassle.

1996 ■ **Senator Robert Dole** resigns to devote full time to pursuit of Presidency.

■ "Unabomber" **Theodore Kaszinski** is caught.

■ Terrorist's bomb devastates U.S. military complex in Saudi Arabia.

■ A bomb goes off during the Centennial Olympics in Atlanta (GA).

1997 ■ A settlement is reached between tobacco manufacturers and attorneys general of several states to recompense for the damages done by cigarettes, but falls apart as Congress attempts to expand it. A second, smaller, agreement is reached.

■ **Independent Counsel Kenneth Starr** continues his *"Whitewater"* investigation of the president. Several indictments are handed down, but none involve the executive branch.

■ Congress and the Justice Department investigate violations of campaign financing laws.

1998   ■**Kenneth Starr** turns his attention to allegations of sexual misconduct and lying under oath charges in depositions given by the president in the Jones lawsuit, even though the Jones case is thrown out of court.

■Kenneth Starr alleges that Clinton committed numerous counts of perjury, subornation of perjury, obstruction of justice and other deeds that warrant impeachment.

■The **House Judiciary Committee** holds hearings on Starr's allegations and votes to submit 4 articles of impeachment to the full house—21 Republicans vote for, 16 Democrats against.

■In the November elections many incumbents, the majority Republicans, lose.

■**Speaker of the House Newt Gingrich** resigns.

■Citing violations of 1991 Gulf War agreement, U.S. and Great Britain launch air attacks against Iraq.

■(December 19, 1998): House votes impeachment of **William Jefferson Clinton** on 2 of 4 counts: perjury and "witness tampering."

■President Clinton's job approval ratings continue to climb higher and be sustained longer than that of any other president in history.

1999
- **Senate's impeachment trial** of President Clinton begins in January and ends in an acquittal.
- U.S. air strikes against Iraq expand.
- A pattern of theft of nuclear secrets (denied by China), dating back to the late 1980s is reported, and Taiwan-born **Wen Ho Lee**, a computer expert at the Los Alamos laboratories, is named prime suspect. He is fired, but never charged.
- President Clinton is found in contempt of court by Arkansas Judge **Susan Webber Wright** for testimony during Jones case.
- The *Independent Counsel Law* is not renewed.
- **Johnny Chung**, a former Democratic fundraiser, reveals that China filtered funds into election campaigns.
- Clinton orders federal agencies to end "racial profiling" in law enforcement.
- Teens **Eric Harris** and **Dylan Kleibold** kill 13, plus themselves, at Colorado's Columbine High School.
- Senate rejects *Nuclear Test Ban Treaty* to condemnation from around the world.
- The U.S. economy rises to new heights.
- U.S. power over the Panama Canal ends.

2000
- **George W. Bush** and **Al Gore** become presidential candidates, with **Dick Cheney** and **Joe Lieberman** as their respective running mates.
- **Hillary Clinton** beats Long Island congressman **Rick Lazio** for the New York Senate seat, becoming the first First Lady elected to an office.
- The Green Party nominates **Ralph Nader** for president.
- **Microsoft** is found guilty of violating the *Sherman Anti-Trust Act.*
- Illinois places a moratorium on executions while other "death penalty" states consider options.
- President Clinton brokers peace talks between Israelis and Palestinians; no agreement is reached.
- Kenneth Starr replacement **Robert Ray** ends *"Whitewater"* hearings, bringing no charges against President or Mrs. Clinton.
- In one of the closest elections in history, **George W. Bush** wins after a controversial Supreme Court ruling gives him the state of Florida and the electoral college vote.

31

The Bush Years

2001 – 2005

2001
- Former senator **John Ashcroft** is named **Attorney General** after bitter Senate confirmation hearings.
- **Colin Powell** and **Condoleezza Rice** become the first Black cabinet members in history.
- FBI agent **Robert Hansen** is arrested as a Soviet spy.
- **President George W. Bush** bars any missile negotiations with North Korea.
- Senate approves a *Campaign Finance Reform* bill to curtail "soft money."
- Senate approves a **$1.3 trillion tax cut,** to be spread over 10 years.
- Census shows minorities outnumber "whites" in most U.S. cities.
- **Louis J. Freeh** resigns as head of the FBI. **Robert S. Mueller III** is later named new head of FBI.
- **Senator James Jeffords** quits the Republican party and becomes an Independent, swinging control of the Senate into Democrats' hands.

■ Both the House and the Senate pass different *"Patients Bill(s) of Rights"* setting standards for health insurers.

■ President Bush and **Russian President Vladimir Putin** agree to cut nuclear arsenals by two-thirds over the next decade.

■ A massive farm subsidy bill, favored by the Democrats, is passed.

■ President Bush agrees to allow limited stem cell research for medical purposes.

■ President Bush announces plans to withdraw U.S. from 1972 *ABM Treaty.*

■ **September 11 (9/11):**

- Terrorists attack on U.S. soil brings destruction of the **World Trade Center (WTC),** and severe damage to **Pentagon,** with close to 3,000 lives lost.

- Immediate steps are taken to calm nation and increase security.

- A plan of retaliation is initiated against attackers, who are identified as members of Al-Qaeda under **Osama bin Laden**, based in Afghanistan.

- Senate votes "all necessary and appropriate force" in new "war on terrorism."

- Arab countries are warned to either join in war on terrorism or face reprisals.

- President demands that the **Taliban,** Afghanistan's ruling party, immediately hand over bin Laden.

- Senate (with presidential approval) passes a financial aid package to troubled U.S. airlines.
- A fund is established to aid victims of the attacks and their families.
- The president establishes the **Office of Homeland Security** to coordinate security and avoid further attacks due to lack of communication.
- U.S. bombers attack Taliban troops in Afghanistan; first reprisal against 9/11.
- Anonymous letters containing the anthrax virus are received in key areas across the country, including the office of **Senate Majority Leader Tom Daschle,** ABC News, CBS News, and in several post offices.
- The attacks cease as abruptly as they began, leaving 5 dead and over 20 stricken. No suspect is accused of the crime.
- **Tom Ridge**, former Governor of Pennsylvania, named to head the Office of Homeland Security.
- Congress passes the *Uniting and Strengthening America by Providing Appropriate Tools Required to Intercept and Obstruct Terrorism (USA PATRIOT) Act,* granting great power and authority to the President and Justice Department in fighting terrorism.
- The Taliban is forced out of power in Afghanistan.

2002

■ **Winter Olympics** in Salt Lake City (UT), test increased high security in the U.S.

■ Senate bill broadens federal participation in education and mandates national testing.

■ In *State of the Union* address, **Bush** cites ongoing "war on terrorism" with emphasis on an "axis of evil" (Iraq, Iran and North Korea).

■ **John Walker Lindh**, an American captured with the Taliban, is tried for "supporting terrorist groups" and "conspiring to kill U.S. citizens." He is sentenced to 20 years to life.

■ The collapse of business giant **Enron** reveals numerous instances of fraud, manipulation and other crimes in numerous large corporations. This causes millions of Americans to lose large sums of money, in many cases, all their retirement monies are lost.

■ *Campaign Reform Bill* is signed curtailing "soft money" contributions.

■ Homeland Security Director **Tom Ridge** announces the *Homeland Security Advisory System* **(HSAS),** a color-coded system designed to let Americans know the perceived level of terrorist threat to the country.

■ A bill to standardize national elections is passed by the Senate.

■ President Bush withdraws U.S. from *ABM Treaty* to allow U.S. to build a revised "Star Wars" defense system.

■ Bush says U.S. will recognize independent Palestinian state only if **Yassir Arafat** is replaced.

■ President Bush calls for a cabinet-level **Department of Homeland Security** that will incorporate diverse elements from many other agencies. This becomes law in November, with Tom Ridge continuing as head of four agencies and 170,000+ employees.

■ Congress approves raising the national debt to **$6.4 trillion.**

■ President Bush announces the first budget deficit in four years.

■ A bill to reform corporations and deter business misconduct is passed.

■ Opposing bills for Medicare drug benefits are presented by the Democrats and Republicans. Both are defeated.

■ Bush calls on the leaders of France, China and Russia to support an attack on Iraq.

■ Bush goes before the U.N. citing Iraq's 11-year flaunting of U.N. authority and production of "weapons of mass destruction" (WMD).

■ Iraq invites weapons inspectors to return. Bush promises to consult Congress before taking any military action against Iraq.

■ Work slowdown by longshoremen shuts down West Coast seaports; losses estimated at $1 billion a day. Bush will invoke *Taft-Hartley Act* to end this.

- North Korea admits violations of pact with U.S. regarding development of nuclear arms.
- Congress backs President Bush's request for use of force in Iraq.
- **Republicans** re-take the **Senate** leading to rare situation of executive and legislative branches being under one party.
- **Senate Majority Leader Trent Lott** makes inappropriate remarks that some see as racist; forced to resign his position, he still remains in the Senate.
- U.S. economy worsens, and President Bush fires **Treasury Secretary Paul O'Neill** and **Lawrence Lindsey, Director of National Economics Council**.

2003
- U.S. proceeds with a massive troop buildup around Iraq, demanding greater proof that Iraq has destroyed all WMD capabilities.
- **President Bush** refuses negotiations with North Korea despite its threat of a (small) nuclear arsenal and its intention to build more.
- The space shuttle *Columbia* crashes, killing all seven crew members. A massive investigation into the cause is started.
- In March, the United States and a coalition of forces mainly from England and Australia, invades Iraq with the goal of disarming **Saddam Hussein** and toppling his regime.

- Within 4 weeks the regime is destroyed with all major members either dead, captured or in hiding. The arduous work of rebuilding Iraq begins.

2004
- New security program requiring fingerprints and photo-IDs for foreign visitors begins.
- Deadly poison Ricin found in **Senator Bill Frist's** office causes shutdown of three government buildings.
- **Massachusetts Supreme Court** rules gay marriage is mandated by state constitution.
- Bush backs a constitutional amendment that will outlaw gay marriage nationwide, but bill never gets out of committee.
- **Senator John F. Kerry** is nominated by Democrats for president. **Senator John Edwards** is running mate.
- Colin Powell, Donald Rumsfeld and Condoleezza Rice, testify before 9/11 Commission looking into intelligence failures prior to the attack.
- U.S. trade deficit reaches record high.
- After admitting to withholding thousands of pages of security documents from 9/11 Commission, Bush Administration turns them over.
- **Specialist Jeremy C. Sivits** becomes the first soldier court-martialed in the **Abu Ghraib** torture scandal. He pleads guilty.

■ The Justice Department reopens the *Emmett Till* murder case.

• 14-year-old Till was lynched in 1955 for whistling at a white girl.

■ The **WWII monument** is formally dedicated.

■ **L. Paul Bremer,** the U.S. administrator in Iraq, formally returns sovereignty to the Iraqis in the person of **Prime Minister Iyad Allawi.**

■ A federal judge in San Francisco declares the 2003 ban on "partial birth" abortions unconstitutional.

■ The **Pentagon** announces the need to extend tours for many soldiers in Iraq to maintain manpower.

■ **President Ronald Reagan** dies from complications of Alzheimer's disease.

■ **Attorney General John Ashcroft** declares that "during war time" the U.S. is *exempt* from having to comply with the **Geneva Convention** or any treaty that bans torture.

■ 9/11 Commission declares there was no connection between that attack and Iraq.

■ The cornerstone is laid for the **Freedom Tower** to be constructed on "Ground Zero" (site of 9/11 WTC attack).

■ **Secretary of Agriculture Ann Veneman** announces plan ending forest protection rules put in place by **President Clinton.**

■ Obesity is declared an illness and thus covered by Medicare.

- Administration refuses funding for **U.N. Population Fund** because some monies go to areas allowing abortion.

- **9/11 Commission** issues report highly critical of U.S. intelligence agencies and government handling of pre-attack intelligence.
  - Urges cabinet-level **Intelligence Director** to oversee all agencies.
  - Bush will, eventually, name **Porter Goss** to the post.

- Former Enron head **Kenneth Lay** is indicted.

- TV star **Martha Stewart** sentenced to five-month prison term for obstruction of justice and perjury.

- Wages are not keeping up with inflation according to the **Bureau of Labor Statistics.**

- Justice Department figures show violent crimes in U.S. at lowest levels in 30 years.

- A federal judge declares parts of *Patriot Act* unconstitutional.
  - Prohibition against unreasonable search and seizure is violated.

- **House Majority Leader Tom DeLay** is rebuked by **Senate Ethics Committee** for putting pressure on fellow senator to vote for Medicare bill.

- He is again rebuked for questionable fund-raising tactics and, still again, for asking federal intervention in Texas dispute of gerrymandering.

■ **Hurricane Ivan** devastates **Alabama** and **Florida Panhandle.**

- Florida alone is hit by four hurricanes, including two within three weeks of each other.

■ **Chief Justice William Rehnquist** announces he has advanced thyroid cancer and is undergoing treatment but continues with his judicial duties.

■ **Mt. St. Helens** (WA) erupts again.

■ First-term cabinet members **John Ashcroft (Attorney General), Donald Evans (Commerce), Colin Powell (State), Spencer Abraham (Energy), Ann Veneman (Agriculture), Rod Paige (Education),** and **Tom Ridge (Homeland Security)** all resign within weeks of the election.

- National Security Advisor Condoleezza Rice is named new Secretary of State (replacing Powell).

■ House Republicans vote to change a rule they had passed requiring leaders and committee chairmen to relinquish their posts in the event of indictment.

- Many see this as a move to protect **Tom DeLay** and certain others who appear to be facing potential indictments.

- Public outcry will force return to original rule.

■ Bush nominates ex-NYC Police Commissioner **Bernard Kerik** as new **Secretary of Homeland Security** (replacing Tom Ridge).

- Subsequent questions on background and character force his withdrawal from consideration.

- **Michael Chertoff** will get post.

■ In effort to control budget growth, President Bush cuts $100 million in aid to global food programs.

■ Bush nominates **Alberto Gonzales** for **Attorney General.**

2005 ■ **President Bush** releases his new budget plan of $2.57 trillion:
- Increases in defense spending.

- Reductions in spending on education, health care, agriculture, transportation and "human services."

- Plan does not include $81 billion Bush asks Congress for separately.

■ Further increases in cost of Medicare drug plan announced.
- Total now set at $724 billion.

■ A bi-partisan group of legislators issues report calling *No Child Left Behind* education plan unconstitutional.

■ Bush nominates **John Bolton,** an official with the State Department, as new U.N. ambassador. A storm of controversy arises because:

- Bolton is an outspoken critic of the U.N. charged with having fired and/or reassigned any employee who disagrees with him, especially in areas pertaining to the Iraq/WMD question.

- When a filibuster threatens to curtail nomination, Bush appoints him during Congressional recess.

■ **Paul Wolfowitz,** seen by many as one of the main architects of the Iraq war, is named to lead the **World Bank.**

■ **Alan Greenspan, Chairman of Federal Reserve Board,** declares budget deficit "unsustainable" and dangerous.

■ Congress rules underage girls must have parental consent to cross state lines for abortions.

■ President Bush announces his Social Security plan.

- Among provisions: benefits to wealthy will be cut to provide long-term funding.

- Critics see this as a step toward making Social Security a "welfare program" for the poor, and, thus, vulnerable.

■ **Amnesty International** names U.S. a major violator of Human Rights, describing **Guantanamo Bay** prison as being "like a gulag."

- ■ The **"Nucular Option"** is avoided
  - Moderate members of both parties hold emergency meeting and reach a compromise.
- ■ The House, over President Bush's threat of a veto, passes a bill to expand stem cell research.
- ■ **W. Mark Felt** reveals himself to be the mysterious **"Deep Throat"** of **Watergate** scandal. He was **Associate Director** of **FBI** at the time.
- ■ **Halliburton,** a company that won a no-bid contract for the rebuilding in Iraq, is accused in Pentagon report of over $1 billion in "questionable" charges.
- ■ *Time* magazine turns over reporter Matthew Cooper's notes on **"Plame Leak"** to **Special Counsel Patrick Fitzgerald,** in charge of the investigation.
- ■ **Supreme Court Justice Sandra Day O'Connor** announces her plan to retire as soon as a replacement can be found.
  - President Bush names **John G. Roberts** as replacement.
  - When Justice Rehnquist dies, Bush moves **Roberts's** nomination to that of **Chief Justice.** He is confirmed in September.
  - Bush will later nominate **White House Counsel Harriet Meiers,** who will withdraw from consideration amid great controversy, and, finally, **Judge Samuel Alito** for the O'Connor slot.

- President Bush signs bill calling for greater domestic oil and gas production and increased use of nuclear power.

- **Hurricane Katrina** hits U.S. with devastating results.

  - Cities of **Biloxi** (MS) and **New Orleans** (LA) are among the hardest hit; New Orleans is all but decimated, with sections like the **Ninth Ward** completely destroyed.

- Oil and gas **refineries** along **Gulf Coast** are **shut down;** some are destroyed.

- U.S. decides to release some of its oil reserves to compensate for loss of production.

  - Apparent slow and inadequate response from the **Federal Emergency Management Agency (FEMA)** to this disaster will cause widespread anger, as well as possibly avoidable chaos, disease and death.

  - **Michael Brown,** FEMA's Director, is replaced.

- Further damage occurs a few weeks later when **Hurricane Rita** hits much of the same area.

- **Hurricane Wilma** cuts a swath of destruction across **Florida,** causing the largest power outages in history.

  - This is the worst year for hurricanes and tropical storms in recorded history, with **28 named storms,** the last of which, does not form until late December (30 days beyond the official end of the Atlantic storm season).

■ The **SEC** announces an investigation into stock dealings of **Senate Majority Leader Bill Frist.**

■ **Tom DeLay** is indicted for "conspiring to violate Texas state election laws" and for "money laundering."

■ Over President Bush's objection, Senate passes law regulating treatment of prisoners, and banning "cruel, inhuman, or degrading treatment."

■ Bush's chief economic adviser **Benjamin Bernanke** is nominated as **Chairman of Federal Reserve Board** (to replace retiring Alan Greenspan).

■ **Venezuelan President Hugo Chavez** leads an anti-Bush demonstration when both are in Argentina for a Latin American summit.

■ In a surprise move, **Senator Harry Reid,** the Democratic minority leader, calls for a closed session of the Senate to discuss failure to investigate faulty intelligence leading up to Iraq war.

■ Senate votes to demand more information about war progress from administration.

■ U.S. **fatalities** in Iraq **exceed 2,000;** more than **13,000** are **wounded.**

  • Both death and casualty tolls continue to climb.

- The Pentagon acknowledges paying Iraqi news outlets to run favorable stories (written by U.S. personnel) in local media.

- **Transportation Security Administration** will allow passengers to carry scissors, small knives and other tools on airplanes.

- 9/11 Commission reports U.S. remains "alarmingly vulnerable to terrorist attacks."

- The *New York Times* sets off a storm of controversy with revelation that President Bush has authorized **National Security Agency (NSA)** to eavesdrop, without a warrant, on thousands of U.S. citizens.

- Extension of *Patriot Act* fails in Congress.

- U.S. trade deficit hits record high of **$68.9 billion.**

- Just days before Christmas, a **three-day strike** by **New York City transit** workers strands millions and stuns retailers.